THOMAS MANN

Thomas Mann

A Study

by

James Cleugh

1933

London: Martin Secker

LONDON : MARTIN SECKER (LTD.) 1933

Ceste insigne fable et tragicque comédie
FRANÇOIS RABELAIS

CONTENTS

PART I: EXPERIENCE

PART II: THE CREATIVE ARTIST

PART I
EXPERIENCE

CHAPTER I

FORMATIVE YEARS

The city of Lübeck stands close to a westerly arm of the Baltic, just south of Kiel Bay. The neighbourhood of this sea, and the commercial spirit born of an excellent harbour, decided from the time of the town's foundation in the twelfth century the character of its inhabitants. As a political and economic power Lübeck dates from its emergence as head of the Hanseatic League of north German trading centres some two hundred years after the incorporation of the city by Henry the Lion, Duke of Saxony. Since then the great industrial families which came to form a patriciate in the place have been distinguished for proper pride, hard heads and good breeding.

Johann Heinrich Mann, who became on the 6th of June, 1875, the father of Thomas Mann, was no exception to this generalisation. He was a grain merchant and a senator of the free city, a strong-minded, sensible gentleman, not without humour, confessing to certain mild literary interests—he even read Zola—and of an extreme elegance in his dress and deportment. In one respect, however, this prominent citizen of a conservative community differed conspicuously from his fellow magnates.

11

He took the course, unusual for a native of Lübeck, of marrying out of his immediate circle. His bride was a lady of mixed German, Portuguese and West Indian blood. Julia da Silva-Bruhn was the child of a marriage between a German planter at Rio de Janeiro and a Brazilian creole. She had been sent over to Germany at an early age to be educated, and grew to be a beauty and an amateur pianist and singer of considerable talent. Thomas Mann was the second son of this unconventional union.

The brothers—Heinrich, the elder by four years, was also destined to become a famous novelist—played together, up to school age, in an old ruined warehouse which stood behind the fine mansion occupied by the wealthy burgher family. They had an East Prussian governess whose loyal, serious and benignant character was, some twenty years later, to be one of the principal ornaments of a literary masterpiece. Thomas learned to love dogs, to detest the militarism of the post-1870 age in which he grew up and to prefer, of the nursery library, stories from Homer and Hans Andersen. A third interest, in opera, was fostered when he inherited from his brother an elaborate toy theatre.

The school period was, on the whole, a gloomy one for the quiet but uncompromisingly independent character which was already formed in the boy. Like Anatole France and Gerhart Hauptmann he thanked God for such brief respites from the labours of education as were available. Prussian state-discipline was then in full force throughout the schools of northern Germany. The idea of rebellion was already finding precociously sarcastic, if secret, expression in the sterner spirits among the pupils subjected to it. Thomas, however, made some friends whose figures were destined for the same sort of preservation as that of his governess. There was a wild and rather grubby young aristocrat who had heard of Nietzsche. There was a handsome young athlete. There were one or two boys who were interested in literature. In this atmosphere the youthful Thomas patiently stagnated, dreamed and slept a good deal, wrote poems and plays and a romance on a Roman stoic theme. On the whole he did badly at school. He calls himself somewhere a man of slow and blunt intelligence. The marvellous intuition that was to make him a great artist was not much use in " form."

But the seaside holidays were oases of a more than usually fruitful kind in the desert of pedagogy. For then the Baltic flowed not only about his limbs but into his heart and into his rapidly developing mind. The sea was to be always for Thomas Mann the symbol of a fascinating, sometimes even, as then, a refreshing philosophical ideal, that of Nirvana. But he puts its first great romantic expression into the mouth of a Schopenhauerian, a hero stricken beyond hope of recovery.

In the year 1890, when Thomas was fifteen, his father died suddenly and the grain business was rather hastily and unprofitably liquidated. The family was left with a comparatively small income. Frau Mann emigrated to Munich, where her artistic leanings might find freer scope, leaving her second son behind in Lübeck to complete his schooling. Heinrich was already in Dresden learning, like Zola, the trade of a bookseller.

During the next three years, until he joined his mother in Munich and entered an insurance office as an unpaid clerk, Thomas Mann's interests were becoming more and more literary. He did little but read. Hans Andersen, with a closer attention to style and structure than his more childish brain had been able to give : Schiller, with an eye to the dramatic possibilities of the toy theatre : Goethe's and Heine's lyrics, which instructed him in the old romanticism, prepared him for the new, and set for ever in his heart the singing note which was never to be quite absent from any of his books.

The first year in the insurance office was also the year of Thomas Mann's first publication, a set of verses printed in a Munich periodical. In spite of Goethe and Heine this lyric did not contain the seeds of future emin-ence. It was clear that Thomas Mann, whatever he was likely to be, would never be a poet in the sense of writing well in metre. But in the insurance office he wrote a love story, *Fallen*, which was in prose, though it had, to be sure, plenty of verses in it. It came out in the same periodical in the year 1894 and brought the author a visit from Richard Dehmel, twelve years Mann's senior and well on the way to becoming the poet that the younger writer was not to be. The admirer of *Fallen* was just then, curiously enough, secretary to the Union of German Fire Insurance Companies. Dehmel never ceased from this moment until his death in 1920 to support Mann in every way he could. He was attracted by the late naturalistic, i.e. Zolaesque, style of this by no means first-class production, which dealt, as might have been expected in view of the author's age, with an aspect of the sexual question, the current male hypocrisy anent female lapses from "virtue." Dehmel saw behind the youthful heat the traces of a polish, an irony, a good taste, which differentiated the little tale from the hundreds of crude imitations and distortions of contemporary French writers then pouring from the German presses. The poet advised Mann to give up insurance and take a course of journalism at the University.

The family resources were sufficient to permit this experiment and also that which Thomas Mann soon afterwards undertook, to wit, a prolonged visit to his brother Heinrich in Rome. Heinrich Mann had gone from Dresden to the office of the celebrated firm of Fischer in Berlin, but was now thinking of becoming a painter. He was already a draughtsman of some ability and hoped in Italy to consolidate his gift. The brothers lived together at No. 34, Via Torre Argentina, near the Pantheon. They spent the summer months at Palestrina, birthplace of the sixteenth-century composer. It was the ancient Praeneste, the resort of Horace and the younger Pliny, and lay in the Sabine hills, some twenty-three miles out of Rome.

The Italian landscape visible from this spur of the Apennines, on a clear day one magnificent riot of colour

and form reaching to the sea at Anzio, or under one of
the wildly lit sunsets of late September a splendid desola-
tion across the Campagna to the very walls of Rome, no
doubt gave the painter Heinrich something to think
about. But his cooler, more fastidious brother found it
difficult to share his enthusiasm. Thomas Mann, with
one exception, long afterwards, when autumnal Venice
got into his blood and the sense of the story he was
writing, never took any particular interest in the luxuriant
panoramas provided by nature. His ascetic eye preferred the sharper, the more mobile and therefore more
mysterious and significant settings of the soul. That hot
and lovely land, which became Heinrich's spiritual home,
spoke to Thomas only of a purely sensuous delight, of
rhetorical emotions alien from the new romanticism he
was slowly formulating. Its clear, lazy day, never visited
by the rousing sting of the northern sea-wind, was for
him only the analogue of a prosaic Latin intellectuality
which could not satisfactorily answer the questions of a
Teutonic moralist.

For Mann's ethical prepossessions were already profound, an essential part of him, though one which was
never to be intolerant or aggressive. Of the huge stock
of artistic wealth that lay in staggering profusion on
every side of the modest dwelling in the Via Torre
Argentina the young moral philosopher remembered
chiefly the painting of the Last Judgment by Michelan-
gelo in the Sistine Chapel. The aesthete in him, however,
which in Thomas Mann means generally, when not the

pure man of letters, the musician, was normally and suitably impressed by the formality, the reserved dignity, the severe economy of antique sculpture. He never forgot, henceforward, what the ancient Greek meant by beauty.

After the first few weeks Thomas Mann was little out of doors. He had no taste for what seemed to him the frivolous adventure of exploring Roman society. He thought the people about him, with their lively manners and dangerous black eyes, superficial and conscienceless. He read and wrote. But not of Italy. He read the Goncourts, especially *Renée Mauperin*. He read Scandinavian literature and revelled again in the bracing atmosphere of the Baltic Sea. He read the great Russians, Turgenev, Tolstoy, Gontcharov. He wrote stories, the long-short continental *Novellen*, which were accepted by important periodicals at home. They were all very distinct advances on *Fallen*. The irony had strengthened and made a happy marriage with nordic sensitiveness, the contours were sharp and accurate, there was a gift for caricature which never overstepped the bounds of decency and good sense. Thomas Mann was already an author and something better. He had become an artist, though not of the type that the Romans, ancient or modern, ever knew.

The unsympathetic Roman scene had driven him back in thought to Germany, to Munich, but most of all to Lübeck. The characters, the environment of these first *Novellen* are predominantly north German. But Mann was meditating, even already writing, a fuller and completer exposition of the Prussian burgher society of the vanishing nineteenth century, the period that had brought him to maturity. When he returned to Munich, after nearly a year's absence, just before the publication in 1898 of his short stories in book form under the title of the first and best of them, *Little Herr Friedemann,* he carried a thick manuscript with him. It was the first bulky instalment of the novel which was to make him famous all over Germany, later all over Europe, to influence heavily the judgment which gave him the Nobel prize for literature in 1929 and to be considered by many critics, even in 1933, the finest work in German prose since Nietzsche.

Buddenbrooks, the long tale of the long decline of an ancient and honourable house of West Prussian merchants very closely resembling the author's own, was not yet finished. Perhaps, in Rome, it could not be. In any case the young, yet mature writer—he was still under twenty-five, but more than old for his age—retraced his steps to Munich, where he was at once provided with an appointment to the staff of *Simplizissimus,* the well-known periodical in which several of his stories had already appeared. One of his colleagues was the young Jakob Wassermann.

The *Simplizissimus* circle has been called a madhouse of wits. It was not over-congenial to Thomas Mann. No doubt the distasteful " South " had too large a share in it for his full sympathy. However, he made friends in it and did not avoid society. But he was happiest in the two rooms which he occupied, apart from his family, and furnished, himself, to his literary satisfaction. There he took up music again, played the violin and the piano, mostly Wagner and Chopin, contemplated the garlanded portrait of Tolstoy which stood on his writing table and worked, under its aegis, hard and harder at *Buddenbrooks*.

A few friends visited him in his retreat. But the friends with whom he passed his most profitable hours were not personally known to him. One was dead, the other had long been silent. The philosophers Schopenhauer and Nietzsche had by now taken the places of Andersen, Heine, Schiller, the Scandinavians and the Russians. Nietzsche came first and stayed for good. But the reader was critical. He would have none of what he called "Cesare Borgia aesthetics and ethics." That was too " southern," though the Nietzschean beast was blond. Mann saw above all else in his new friend the self-fighter, the stoic, the disciplinarian. Once and for all the facile romanticism, " self-expression," the affirmation of the ego, whatever its nature, in and out of season, died in him at the feet of the mightiest and loneliest literary personality then alive, though mortally sick and broken, in Europe. As for Schopenhauer, Mann's intoxication with the theories of pessimism expressed by that profound intellect was as complete as Wagner's had been. The shadow of *The World as Will and Idea* is dark over the second volume of *Buddenbrooks*.

Mann's year of military service was now due. Just before he reported, not too enthusiastically, at headquarters, he finished his great manuscript, which had taken him three years to write, and despatched it to Messrs. Fischer in Berlin, registering it as of the value of one thousand marks, whereat the clerk is related to have twitched a humorous lip.

The term of army service was a short one. It was passed chiefly in the infirmary. Thomas Mann developed severe and obstinate ankle inflammation, which made drill and marching out of the question. The family doctor consulted the regimental. Thomas was given his freedom and assigned to the category of " last resorts."

He had corresponded with Messrs. Fischer from the infirmary. The publishers had requested the young author to cut the two volumes of *Buddenbrooks* down to one. Mann refused point-blank. He had scarcely left the army when he received the reply from Berlin. Messrs. Fischer would publish *Buddenbrooks* forthwith, and in two volumes.

CHAPTER II
SUCCESS AND EXPLORATION

Buddenbrooks was published at the end of 1900, with the imprint of 1901. The new century was fairly launched, and with it a new writer who was to reach the very front rank of European men of letters. In a few months Thomas Mann began to savour the heady fruits of elevation to that literary purple which means a good deal more in Germany than elsewhere. The masses acclaimed him at once as the " teacher " which the first-class German artist, from Goethe downwards, has always been assumed to be. As a true German Mann accepted the designation with pleasure, in good and justified faith. Not that *Buddenbrooks* was in any very direct sense didactic. It was not obviously a " story with a moral." But it was a story written by a moralist, and that was enough for Germany. The idea behind this word was for Germans, as for most Europeans, far broader and deeper, and at the same time far simpler, than the English connotation. It went back to Theophrastus and the old French sense as revived by Nietzsche, the sense which had been epitomised in La Bruyère. It meant no more than an investigator into the problem of good and evil. But it meant everything that an investigator can or should be. It implied impartiality, so introducing a direct anti-thesis to the English " moralist " who is usually under-stood to be a bigot. It implied also scientific acumen, philosophic depth, imaginative idealism, above all a passionate and serious concern—what Plato would have called σπουδαιότης—with Wellsian " first and last things."

Thomas Mann's success with *Buddenbrooks* meant that he was publicly presented with the title of " moralist " in this sense. The experience drew him out of the sphere, which was showing some signs of becoming a vicious circle, of that defiant melancholy which always affects exceptional minds in their first youth and is partly a simple pain of growth and partly an impatience with that process.

By the time the two-volume novel had gone into a second edition at the end of the year Mann felt the access of power of two kinds. Power over his fellow-country-men and power within himself to follow his star. With characteristic deliberation he began to labour slowly and surely on its track.

The critics on this occasion, as so often in the case of work destined for a long life, had been anticipated by the public. They now fell into step behind the main body of appreciation. It began to be stated on high authority that never before in German literature had there appeared such a perfect photograph. That never before had a photograph so conveyed the effect of a noble painting. And that never before had a painting aspired so nearly, in its technique and in its content, to the condition of the greatest music.

It was the photographic quality of *Buddenbrooks* that, as time went on, raised a storm in the teacup of Lübeck. Important citizens complained that they were perfectly recognisable in cruel caricatures. The non-resident author was vindictively attacked, though the opposition, unlike that which had nearly put Ibsen out of business on similar grounds forty years before, was never much more than regional, even almost entirely local. It was not until close on five years had passed that any concrete action was taken. But at last the Lübeck faction went to law. In the year 1904 a certain " Bilse," the pseudonym of an army officer, had published a *roman à clef*, a scurrilous account of garrison-town life in the form of a novel, into which he had introduced well-known characters in veils of positively gauzy transparency. The book was ill-written, ill-natured and ill-making, as the London slang of 1920 would have had it, but it achieved, as such productions generally do achieve, a certain success. Thomas Mann was accused, during the libel action brought by the citizens of Lübeck, of having adopted the Bilsian formula in *Buddenbrooks*. The charge was, of course, quite ludicrous. The popular author had no difficulty in defending the right of an artist to use, as Goethe and Turgenev did, his own experience. It was good " naturalism." Nor did Mann hesitate to point out the logical inconsistency of the prosecution. If the author's treatment of a virtuous citizen was as damagingly malicious as was alleged, how on earth could the virtuous citizen recognise himself or be recognised by others? The case was dismissed. The fact was that most of the business people in *Buddenbrooks* were quite respectable and charming, though ironised. The affair, however, enabled Mann to clarify in his own mind certain principles of artistic procedure, which he took the trouble to publish in 1906 under the title *Bilse and I*, and to perceive how his gift for caricature could be cultivated to a deeper level.

Between the time of the publication of *Buddenbrooks* and the appearance, in 1903, of a new volume of *Novellen*, to which the first story of the six gave its title of *Tristan*, the author's literal, though not precisely spiritual, home was Munich. Through the gay streets and the great sunny squares, in and out of the Springlike atmosphere of the cafés and the taverns passed the figures of many living men who were making aesthetic history. Frank Wedekind, Franz Werfel, Richard Dehmel, Eduard Count Keyserling, Friedrich Huch. And for Thomas Mann, mingling with the exuberant forms of his contemporaries, passed, too, the phantoms of the dead. Wagner, who had made the music that sounded most deeply in the heart of the young writer; Fontane, the early weary decadent, the modest admirer of hearty lieutenants, the wise and witty stylist; it was Fontane, old Fontane, as Mann affectionately called him in a later critical essay, who had trained the new author in the use of perhaps his most effective weapon, that two-edged irony in which the pupil had surpassed the teacher. Then there was E. T. W. Hoffmann, of the *Tales*, who had shown the seeker after a new romanticism that the wildest fantasy could be combined with the soberest realism; Flaubert, the stories of whose almost incredibly deliberate workmanship—five days to write a page, eight hours to correct five pages—encouraged a writer whose own genius was already of the type which Carlyle had defined as an infinite capacity for taking pains. He was haunted by Schiller, who fought, as Mann was to show in a later *Novelle*, even harder than Flaubert; by Ibsen, whose aphorism, " To write is to go to law with oneself," stood on the title-page of *Tristan*, where the action was brought by burgher against artist, by Lübeck against Thomas Mann; and always by Goethe, Schopenhauer, Nietzsche.

One of the new stories in *Tristan, The Way to the Churchyard*, was dedicated to a close friend of Mann's, one Arthur Holitscher, a writer who subsequently became a prominent communist. But Herr Holitscher's pleasure at this compliment was mitigated by the personal reaction of an altogether different kind which he experienced in reading *Tristan* itself, the first story in the volume. A protagonist in this narrative, the aesthete and author Detlev Spinell, who cuts a figure which can hardly be described for the average mind as anything but contemptible, appeared definitely to resemble the gentleman to whom *The Way to the Churchyard* had been inscribed. Holitscher remembered with indignation the sequel to an occasion upon which he had called on Thomas Mann, finding him at his music, and passed some hours in his company pleasantly enough. When the visitor had left, however, and had gone some way along the street, he happened to glance back, no doubt with a certain reverence, at his late host's window, which was easily visible from where he stood. To his profound stupefaction and keen resentment, he perceived that Thomas Mann was examining him through an opera glass.

The incident led to an exchange of letters. Mann protested that, as a provincial like himself would naturally do, he was merely observing the picturesque bustle of the southern metropolis. He added that Detlev Spinell resembled Thomas Mann far more than Arthur Holitscher : and that in any case a writer was entitled to draw upon his experience. The last two arguments he was to use again in the " Bilse " case. But the aggrieved party was convinced only of the celebrated Mannian irony, which he believed he had detected in his friend's letter of explanation. He did not, however, as those of Lübeck did later, proceed to " take steps." The matter was dropped. But the episode deserves to be recorded, whatever the precise grounds for its occurrence may have been, for the light it throws upon the first-hand methods, at this date, of the West Prussian exile.

The critics took *Tristan* to their bosoms more promptly than they had taken *Buddenbrooks*. This time they outstripped the public. The stories moved in an atmosphere stranger to the average German than that of the patrician mercantile circles of the novel. The principal figures were all neurotic in one way or another and the fastidious prose was rather their vehicle than that of the many saner characters. A pitiful drunkard whom Dostoievsky might have signed, a frail Tchehovian aesthete, a doomed, fantastic invalid, a nervous child in the grotesque body of a colossus, a grandiloquent fanatic who had to acknowledge humiliation and defeat; such were the twilight voices that gave the pages of *Tristan* too close an air for the burghers who had rejoiced in the spacious and vivid scenes of *Buddenbrooks*. Yet the younger inhabitants of Germany and most of the professional critics acclaimed one tale of the six a masterpiece.

Tonio Kröger, which bore a special dedication to the author's friend Kurt Martens, was Mann's own favourite, and it is not difficult to see why. The title-rôle was sustained by a hero who might pass for a very tolerably accurate self-portrait. Lonely, ascetic, fully conscious, without arrogance, rather with despair, of his own genius, racked by desires impossible either to satisfy or to repress, one of those ill-starred dual natures, half *bourgeois* and half artist, which for the author had come to symbolise an eternal strife between the world and the spirit, Tonio Kröger, with his significantly contradictory, Italo-German name, stands well enough for Thomas Mann himself at this period.

In the course of the story this character, on a visit to his native town, is detained by the police. It was a case of mistaken identity. But the artist—Kröger is a writer by profession—is not surprised. Is not a respectable citizen who has strayed into Bohemia in reality a sort of criminal? Is not an artist far more likely to throw over social traces than a business man? The lives of artists are rarely edifying. That of one of the greatest ever born in Germany, Richard Wagner, whose art had always had a profound influence upon Thomas Mann himself, scarcely repaid even a reverent attention.

This event of fiction, like so many in Mann's books, was founded on actual fact. The already celebrated author had been detained, himself, while on a visit to Lübeck, the police believing him to be a certain notorious swindler who was understood to be passing through the neighbourhood. The irony of the situation was not lost upon the master of irony. He never forgot that, for a moment, artist and criminal had seemed to honest men to have coalesced in his own person.

The year 1905 was an important one for Thomas Mann. He was just thirty. His literary renown was established beyond dispute. He was writing a play, *Fiorenza*, which was intended to eclipse all his previous performances. And he was in love.

Women had played no very conspicuous part in his life hitherto, though each of his three published books showed that he understood them as well as could be expected in the case of a writer so essentially male, and in fact better than many professed feminists. The vampire in *Little Herr Friedemann*, the ingenuous and impulsive Toni Buddenbrook, and the calm intellectual, Lisaweta Ivanovna, in *Tonio Kröger*, were three types of the younger representatives of the sex that everyone could recognise as true and vital. A story in the *Tristan* volume had been dedicated to an English girl whom he met at a hotel in Florence in his Italian days. But the association would appear to have been what used to be called an innocent one. It was, at all events, brief and never renewed.

Thomas Mann married, in the year 1905, Fräulein Katja Pringsheim, the daughter of an eminent professor of mathematics and amateur of Wagnerian music. The lady was herself a mathematician as well as a beautiful brunette. The connection brought Mann once more into close relations with the burgher circle from which he had parted, but which he had never since, at any rate in thought, quite abandoned, when he left the insurance office for Rome. The Pringsheims were decidedly more intellectual than the Buddenbrooks. But there were no artists in the family. The marriage was and remained a great success.

The following year was the witness of a far more unexpected event. The author of up-to-date narrative fiction published a play about Savonarola and Lorenzo the Magnificent. There was, no doubt, much of late Renaissance Florence in early twentieth century Munich. The scene of the story which Mann had dedicated to the English lady-resident in the Florentine hotel was set in the modern German city. That tale might now be considered as forming in certain respects a preliminary study to the larger work issued in 1906. Artists, most of them literally painters, of whom there were just then a very large number in the Bavarian metropolis, are prominent in the play, while the *Novelle*, too, has much to say of them. They figure in both cases, though the first picture is a more sympathetic one, as a group of gay and cynical craftsmen, the brilliant but superficial mechanics viewed by the Philistine, rather than the almost hieratic characters created by the average romantic mind. They are the typical " Bohemians," with whom Mann had to be only too well acquainted for professional purposes in Munich and whom he could not help despising. It was something, a psychological compensation, an escape from the burden of this particular experience, to get that scorn sublimated into the noble periods of *Fiorenza*.

The typical artists in the play are such as Aldobrandino who, quite in the spirit of 1930, is much less interested in the Madonna than in the technical problem of the management of reds and greens in her gown, such as Ghino, who would as soon illustrate Boccaccio as St. Thomas Aquinas. The writers, the " humanists " of the day, are of the same general type. Poliziano derides moral decency ; Pico della Mirandola advocates its revival on the ground that men capable of so ridiculous an undertaking will prove that Italy can still breed heroes. This was the sort of talk that Thomas Mann had heard in the cafés of the Frauenplatz and that had sickened him of the doctrine of art for art's sake.

Heinrich Mann was an authority on both sides of the Renaissance medal, even if his Renaissance was nearer the baroque than the height of the period. Although Thomas was never in the least under the influence of Heinrich, any more than Heinrich was ever under his, the Italian conversations must have contributed to the manufacture of *Fiorenza*, and especially to the figure of Lorenzo, who bears more than one trait of the brilliant elder brother.

Deeper in the pages of the drama lay Thomas Mann's own spiritual experience of the last ten years. Out of the indecision and the torment of internal strife had come the strength to create and the pride of achievement. Savonarola and Lorenzo, though both were physically and mentally sick, were both heroes. They were artists of a calibre different from that of Aldobrandino or Pico, or the vociferous modern frequenters of the Munich cafés.

The play was duly produced in the city where the author had chosen to live and was even given a trial by Max Reinhardt in Berlin. But it appeared at a moment which, however congenial to Heinrich Mann, was unsuited to the genius of his brother. Munich was in the full flood of a romantic revival of the cloak and sword variety. It was believed at first by the melodramatists that their flamboyant banner had been favoured by a new and formidable ally. In the theatre, however, they discovered their mistake. Dramatically *Fiorenza* is very playable and has some fine moments. But it resembles neither the comedies of Lope de Vega nor " Don Juan " and might just as well be recited as acted. Essentially, it is a piece for the study. The volatile and optimistic south German audience of 1906 rejected its tragic debate. It was left to the embittered Viennese of 1918 to understand and applaud, for the first time in a theatre, the stern ethical sentiment that underlay the splendid prose. In the Austrian metropolis, too, as in fifteenth century Florence, an epoch devoted to social pleasures and the cultivation of the beautiful was passing, was in fact already being replaced by an age of poverty and pain, favourable to a triumph of the religious impulse over the cultural. But the once wealthy patrons of the theatre in Vienna were now too reduced in numbers and fortune to ensure any drama, however congenial to them, a long run.

The comparative ill-success of Mann's play in stage production ended by confirming his distrust of " theatre " as a medium for his particular genius. Even in his early teens the elaborate toy he had inherited from Heinrich had been mostly used for the setting forth of operas. He never wrote another drama and still maintains that, quite apart from commercial considerations, a scene from a novel touches truth more closely than any stage script. Mann's interest in the theatre became, after *Fiorenza*, more and more confined to the psychology and sociological effects of the actor type. His own leisurely and deliberate spirit is undoubtedly far better absorbed from an armchair at home than from a stall in a playhouse.

Those, in fact, who read *Fiorenza* without running to the auditorium saw that Thomas Mann had advanced another astonishing step in his triumphant career. The work definitely enhanced the reputation of this author of rich surprise packets. When, three years later, a book by Thomas Mann even more utterly unexpected appeared all Germany was impatient and ready for any marvel that its new magician cared to produce.

A Munich painter, one of those whose pictures conveyed something more than manual dexterity, had presented Mann with a canvas representing the youthful figure of a Spanish king, seated upon a magnificent throne in a Renaissance setting, in a posture of despair, his face buried in his hands. There were no other persons portrayed in this composition, which suggested effectively the lonely isolation of royalty.

The mind of Thomas Mann was by birth, traditions and choice an aristocratic one. He was already deeply impressed by the remoteness of aristocratic feeling from the temper of the mass of mankind. He knew that the idea of aristocracy was unsympathetic to the age in which he lived. In south Germany the spirit of independence of dynastic authority to be found in artistic and intellectual circles was the adult and powerful form of the precociously scornful sentiment he had encountered, approved and actually himself fostered at his Prussian school. But Mann had never been a conventional democrat. Of the mental experiences from which arose the work, *Royal Highness*, in the beginning somewhat of a riddle to his critics and readers, faith in the man of breeding as the natural leader of humanity was perhaps the first. But a patrician is a lonely man. If he is also in any sense an artist, as he must be if he is to rule, that is, educate his people, he will be thrice as lonely. For the artist, Mann has written, is a cross between Lucifer and a clown.

The author's own bitterness of isolation, that had begun in Lübeck among the Philistines, continued in his dreary Roman exile and reached its height at Munich, among artists who were only too artistic. But it had been dispelled by his marriage. Love, he found, as so many had found before him, had solved the problem, for the moment at any rate. Life, which had been so difficult, began to seem easy. A mood utterly different from any in which his previous works had been conceived characterised the new novel. It was a comedy, a modern fairy tale of bogeys laid and obstacles smoothed away by that smiling power which works the only real magic in the world. The new gaiety that informed this period of the life of Thomas Mann astonished people who had not thought him capable of such a thing. Humour had never been far below the surface, indeed often conspicuously above it, in even the most tragic of his previous tales. But such humour, zestful and light though it frequently was, had less continuity, less depth and above all less delicacy and charm than the gleaming summer of *Royal Highness*. Thomas Mann was unequivocally happy for the first time in his not yet very long life.

He reprinted a number of his *Novellen*, including two new narratives, one of which, *The Famished*, is significant for its suggestion of the universal misdirection of envy. A bored guest leaves an entertainment for which the beggar outside is, absurdly in the guest's view, languishing. That the beggar is on the wrong tack, as Mann himself had been until his marriage, seems to be the implication.

By 1909 the sceptic was beginning to find scepticism vulgar and to profess a new belief in life, the ironist had consented to become benevolent, the lonely king had dried his tears and lifted his head to order an enchanting world.

Almost at once an event of tragic horror took place in Mann's own family circle. His second sister Carla was an actress, not of outstanding talent and consequently given to fits of depression which she was still too young to resist. A rising industrialist, not much older than herself, was in love with her and had proposed marriage, which had been agreed to. But the merchant had reason to believe that his betrothed was unfaithful to him. He called at Frau Mann's residence and demanded an explanation. The girl fled from the room and poisoned herself in another part of the house.

Happiness is not necessarily an illusion because sorrow is continually interrupting and even corrupting it. But sorrow may have the effect of turning a man's thoughts, consciously or subconsciously, to the question of illusion in its general aspect. The philosopher of life must take account of it. And he may even end by regarding it as, to some extent, desirable. Carla Mann was an actress.

Those who act on the stage minister to a widespread and morally justifiable need of mankind. They are artists. But those who act off the stage, while their activities have less, or it may be sometimes no such justification, are also in their way artists. An artist may be a king. But Mann had already reflected, at the police station in Lübeck, that he may also be, under certain conditions, a criminal.

Whatever the value of these considerations may be it is a fact that a part of Thomas Mann's literary work between the years 1910 and 1912 was the composition of a first instalment of a book purporting to be the memoirs of a " swell mobsman." The instalment, which remained an instalment, was not published until 1922. Completion was interrupted by the war and also by certain labours which were to bear more important and more immediate fruit. Of *The Confessions of the Archswindler Felix Krull*, as the memoirs were entitled, it is only necessary to record here that the work reflected a particular change of outlook in the author, an interest in the philosophy of illusion for its own sake, which had been absent, even, by implication, decried in his earlier works. There he had been concerned only to insist upon the eradication of hypocrisy. Here he seems to find a value, a decidedly unconventional value, in histrionic fraud. The value he found was calculated, indeed, to horrify, though Mann here as always wrote soothingly enough, the upholders of a dogma that thirty or forty years ago had been a heresy, but was now a tradition.

SUCCESS

The literary naturalism deriving from Zola, which had been the fashion in Mann's first youth, was more than a style. It was a habit of thought, a rejection of social compromise, a devotion to " nature " as the materialisation of simplicity and logic. Thomas Mann had subscribed to this doctrine as much as he ever subscribed to any, though his attitude to its onslaughts on the *bourgeois* was always equivocal. But in *Felix Krull* his allegiance, such as it was, became a faint and formal one. It had far more to do with style than with intellectual conviction. " Nature " has come to seem almost grotesque. The memoirs turned out to be actually a flash in the pan. But the flash was a brilliant one, as a post-war generation, more attuned to such social improprieties, was to find.

The work which had been one of the reasons for the breaking off of the composition of *Felix Krull* when the eponymous hero was still at the threshold of manhood, was *Death in Venice*. It was a rather longer *Novelle* than Mann usually wrote, approaching forty thousand words, yet it scarcely reached the proportions of a novel in the English sense. But it made more impression on the public and on the critics than anything of his since *Buddenbrooks*.

If *Royal Highness* may be considered as the finely articulated expression of the first gay rapture of love, *Death in Venice* was such a masterpiece as the lover who has penetrated to the sober serenity of bliss behind the intoxicating storm may write. The determinism of Friedrich Nietzsche, whose thought was as powerfully stimulant as ever, and perhaps more deeply digested in Mann during these years than in early youth ; the rejection of " naturalism " in the sense of a photography of the comparatively banal, intellectually facile if difficult in execution ; the conception of beauty as a remote ideal to be pursued rather than possessed ; a reading of Plato with which the antique statues seen in Rome may have had something to do ; a vision of the abyss which yawns beside the path even of the successful artist and psychologically balanced man of the world ; such mental adventures could be discerned, some clearly, some more dimly, as a prelude to the clear, dreamful ease, so classically restrained in its quiet harmonies, of the mature art that constructed *Death in Venice*, the only long work of Thomas Mann that looks to the soft, to the dangerously seductive south, here the setting for a last tragic scene in the life of a man of northern blood.

Frau Thomas Mann's health necessitated, in the year 1912, a visit to a locality in some ways hardly less exotic than Venice. This was Davos in eastern Switzerland. Her husband's impressions of the place and more particularly of life in the sanatorium which his wife inhabited, led him to conceive the plan of a new book. It was to be a comedy, narrative in form, of slight and perhaps fanciful content and texture. That fascination by death which had been the motive of the tragic *Death in Venice* was to assume a comic form and found a grotesque story as a pendant to its predecessor, like the " satyr-plays " of the Greek tragedians. But circumstances the sinister reverse of slight and fanciful were profoundly to modify this original scheme. Thomas Mann had only been for some months at work upon it, in his deliberate way, and had meanwhile published a new volume of *Novellen*, bound up with and called after his most successful of former years, *Tonio Kröger*, when the alarm of war set his mind moving in far different directions.

CHAPTER III
WARTIME

THE European conflict of 1914-1918 was as little anticipated by Thomas Mann as by most men of letters in
Germany. He took, at that time, very little interest in
politics. But he was patriotic in the sense that he believed that the frontiers of his country conserved a
spiritual content that was valuable, not only for Germans
but for Europe. He could not remain, like Gerhart
Hauptmann, to pace upon the mountains overhead and
hide his face among the stars. Hauptmann, the only contemporary German writer whose stature could for a
moment be considered to exceed Mann's, did not inter-
rupt his magisterial output in the least from 1914 to 1918.
And his imaginative work had very little to do with the
war. Thomas Mann, on the other hand, published no
imaginative literature during the four fatal years.

He was still only thirty-nine years old, thirteen years
younger than the great Silesian. His mind was more
multiple, more specifically and practically intellectual.
He felt that he had a part to play. It was an extraordinarily difficult part. But the level-headed ironist and
staunch champion of German culture played it with
matchless dexterity and dignity.

WARTIME

His relations with the armed forces of the German Empire had been, as was noticed in an earlier chapter, the briefest possible for a man of his nationality. He had not shown himself to be of the physical stuff of which literal soldiers are made. He was now, in point of fact, certified by an army doctor who happened to have read his books as permanently unfit for military service, less on physical grounds indeed than owing to the doctor's enthusiastic estimate of his intellect. It was a typically German concession, which is, one realises with shame and a sympathy for Mann's own view of the German spirit, unthinkable in any other country.

He was in Brussels in 1915, in connection with a production in that city of his play *Fiorenza*. The Belgian capital was then, of course, under German martial law. Mann had thus an opportunity of observing his countrymen on active military service and he has left some fugitive sentences on record which express, with some irony, the detachment he felt among these decorated warriors, one of whom actually addressed him some weeks later in a written communication which opened with the startling words, " Herr War Comrade ! "

But Thomas Mann, in spite of his detestation of the exaggerated military discipline of a political kind which had darkened his schooldays and later aroused the sarcastic comments of the Munich intellectuals, believed in a strict military discipline of the soul. He came, on the father's side, of stern Prussian stock. That he had not forgotten this is often evident in the works written prior

41

THOMAS MANN

to 1914, especially *Death in Venice*, whose aesthete-hero
is by no means only incidentally a stoic. Nor had his
spiritual father, Friedrich Nietzsche, any less influence.
What was soldierly in the ideas and in the character of
that philosopher had sunk deep in Mann. The similari-
ties between war and art, the necessity for faith, for enthusiasm, for organisation, for the stiff upper lip, had
escaped him as little as they had his heroes Flaubert and
Schiller.

In August 1914 Mann put aside the literary work of
an imaginative character upon which he was engaged.
It comprised *Felix Krull* and the notes which were
rapidly growing under his hand for the " sanatorium "
novel. He turned to some memoranda he had also collected for a work—it was originally intended to be a
novel—upon one of the most brilliant soldiers of all time,
Frederick the Great. The idea had been to make the
main interest psychological. But the stress of the moment modified this project. The inchoate historical novel
became the complete historical essay. It was a serious
contribution to the study of politics and war in the
eighteenth century in Europe and it was also an excellent
manual for the patriotic fighting man of the Germany of
1914. Messrs. Fischer of Berlin published this memoir,
with two other articles of equally timely and more direct
appeal, in the April following such an August as Frederick, too, had faced at the beginning of the greatest
military exploit of his life.

By this time there was war in Germany as well as

outside it. Intellectual factions were rife. Mutual accusations of treachery flew about as they did in all the belligerent countries. Thomas Mann did not escape. In spite of the true and deep patriotism which informed his literary utterances, perhaps because that patriotism was truer and deeper than and therefore not so explicit and vociferous as that of others, he was arraigned for shirking the duties of citizenship. And also for carrying them out only too well by not joining a strong section of opinion in pro-Entente propaganda.

This comedy of errors had to be dealt with somehow. The mind of Thomas Mann was too lively and even pugnacious to disdain defence. He was drawn into a political arena, where, as might have been anticipated, he found his own brother against him. Heinrich Mann prided himself upon being a good democrat, a good European and an immoralist. For him the versatile, cosmopolitan and sceptical man of the High, or better still the Baroque Renaissance was the human ideal. Heinrich was " progressive," enlightened, in Thomas's view somewhat irresponsible, and very eloquent, particularly when Germany was in the pillory. He and his friends were really the main body of the opposition which Thomas Mann had to meet. The flank attacks were less damaging, depending as they did upon a view of patriotic obligation and upon a conception of the function of the artist at a moment of national crisis which most reflective persons, in time of peace, would be ready to condemn as superficial and short-sighted. Thomas Mann could refuse, with reason, to join in hymns of hate and self-righteousness. And he did so, entrenching himself firmly within a moral and psychological approval in principle rather than charging to the cheer of a myopic rationalisation in practice.

But the intellectuals, with their honeyed rhetoric of peace and fraternity—which did not, apparently, extend to the stubborn *fratres* of their leading lights—were a harder nut to crack. Thomas Mann cracked it with the aid of his old friends Schopenhauer, Nietzsche, Wagner and the Russians, Tolstoy, Turgenev and Dostoievsky. Fraternity, ran the pith of his argument, comes from within the soul. It cannot be imposed by force of the reason of the " humanist."

The wordy battle lasted as long as that which was being waged with guns and bombs. It was not until 1918 that Mann felt his position secure enough to launch in *Reflections of a Non-Political Man* the substance of his apologia and the story of that private struggle which paralleled the public strife within and without the frontiers of his country.

The experiences of these years, during which the lonely figure that had descended from the mountains of the Muse to the dust of conflict maintained itself so stoutly, were exhausting. They certainly assisted Mann to formulate his intellectual attitude more definitely than before the war and in the *Reflections* to let the public frankly into many of the secret places of a heart they could not finally help admiring. But it may be doubted whether the stimuli of this trying period equalled in creative force the Lübeck years, the Roman holiday for which so many Heinrichian illusions had been butchered, the literary successes and encounters with the wits in Munich, the marriage to the mathematically-minded fairy princess, the tragic death of Carla Mann.

There was, however, an incident in the year 1915 which made a profound impression in intellectual circles both in Germany and in France. This was the open letter of Romain Rolland, the winner of the Nobel prize for literature of that year, to Gerhart Hauptmann, the only other eminent European who stood *au dessus de la mêlée*, on the subject of the burning of Louvain. The last instalment of Rolland's vast epic narrative, *Jean-Christophe*, the biography of an imaginary German musician, had been published in 1912. The letter turned the minds of many literary men in Germany, whether they had previously read Rolland or not, to the perusal or re-perusal of this great essay on the psychology of the artist. It was a topic peculiarly interesting to Thomas Mann, the more so in view of his now twelve-year-old study of the same phenomenon in *Tonio Kröger*, one of the most successful of his shorter tales. *Jean-Christophe* put the case for the international character of art far more persuasively than had Heinrich Mann. In his brother music went a good deal deeper than a passion merely secondary to letters. As for Schopenhauer and for Nietzsche the organisation of sound had for Thomas Mann a metaphysical significance. The dark agonies of Rolland's robust hero, with all that philosophic warrior's psychological distance from the delicate pessimism of Tonio Kröger, could be well understood by the lonely champion of a new romanticism. Yet Mann discerned French prejudice behind the cosmopolitan veil. He could not agree with Rolland's notion of a co-existent true and false Germany. He could only accept with many reservations the noble conclusion of *Jean-Christophe*. But the *Reflections* and all Mann's subsequent works owe an appreciable proportion of the depth of their argument to the author of *Au Dessus de la Mêlée* and *Le Quatorze Juillet*. Nor is it unlikely that the ideas of M. Rolland assisted the compounding of brotherly strife which followed 1918. Thomas Mann emerges from the war period far more of a European, though still an unrepentant German, than he entered it, even though *Buddenbrooks* had been very little less a novel for Europe than for Germany.

CHAPTER IV
EVEN TENOUR

THE grim years that followed the armistice were preceded by a few months in which a simple relief that the orgy of blood-letting was at an end predominated over misgiving, shame and anger in Germany. Thomas Mann had inhabited with his wife and children, since 1908, the small country town of Tölz on the river Isar, the rapid stream once celebrated by the Scottish poet Thomas Campbell, not far from Munich. By the end of the year 1918 Mann's controversial activities, which since the beginning of the war had been political in a sense never hitherto directly applicable to him, had died down. With the external strife of the German nation the internal disputes in which he had been engaged seemed to be over. He was reconciled with Heinrich. No one now reproached him with being either a bad or a good citizen. The moment was favourable to recreation and the intellectual stress and nervous strain which had gone to the making of the *Reflections* imperatively demanded a rest.

He took a good many long country walks with his dog Bauschan, *anglicé* "Lump," a by no means pedigree quadruped, but a good hunter and an interesting charac-

ter. There were some odd occurrences on these expeditions, which led Bauschan's master to take up the study
of zoology and animal behaviour. Since his childhood
he had loved dogs. In mature manhood the riddle of
their psychology began to attract his attention. The
Mann public was in for another surprise.

In 1919 the novelist of commercial and artistic declines
and falls, the dramatist of a Renaissance antithesis, the
author of a modern fairy tale five hundred pages long,
the brilliant historical memorialist, the uncompromising
critic of himself and of society, published an idyll. The
tone was idyllic, but the realism was masterly and the
scientific observations and deductions, a new feature in
Mann's work, might have been made by a trained professional investigator. This composition was entitled
Herr und Hund and was translated into English four years
later as *Bashan and I*. It was not the first work of Mann
to appear in an English dress. A version of *Royal Highness* had been published by Messrs. Sidgwick and Jackson
in 1916. But the reception of the shorter work, due as
much, perhaps, to the attraction of a subject congenial
to a nation of amateurs in the canine as to any widespread
realisation of the standing of the writer, was enthusiastic.

Those mental qualities, for example, humour, sympathy and scientific curiosity, which lead a complex
nature like Mann's to interest itself in an apparently
simple object, such as a short-haired mongrel setter, or
any animal, conduct also to the appreciation of a similarly
elementary-looking phenomenon, the human infant. The

distinguished *prosateur*, before the year was out, was again before a bewildered audience with a second idyll, this time actually in hexameters, celebrating his latest born of five. The *Gesang vom Kindchen*, or "Song about Childie," was not a masterpiece. The medium prevented that. Thomas Mann could never write good verse. There had been hexametrical rhythms in the prose of *Master and Dog*. They had not made it anything less than very good prose. But strict verse hexameters were beyond him and indeed he did not attempt them. The pattern was Goethe's *Hermann und Dorothea*, which the aged metrist Voss had condemned *in toto* from the technical point of view. But as a record of experience the "Song about Childie" presented the author of genuine masterpieces in still another new light, that of the proud parent in a time when most parents were mourning and the innocence of childhood had an interest even more pathetic than usual. Most men have become fathers sooner or later. But only a limited number have seen their child grow against a background such as obtained in post-war Germany. Still fewer have seen, as Thomas Mann, thinking of Goethe's young lovers in the stormy glare of the French Revolution, saw, the dramatic values, the significance for the comprehension of life, of the situation. And perhaps no one but Mann, or Goethe, could have made literature of it. All the same, the "Song" would have been better in prose.

By 1920 the brief period of respite from wartime agonies and horrors, the period which had produced the "idylls," had passed into the beginnings of the scarcely less harrowing tumults of "The Peace." Mann's position as the second most admired writer in Germany and certainly the most practically intellectual, was a prominent one. No doubt his countrymen expected him to enter the arena once more. He was well aware of the real responsibility he had, almost that of a ruler, certainly that of a public sage. He was proud of it and glad to exercise it. But he did not feel in the least pontifical. And he had determined, after 1918, to have nothing more to do with politics.

Ever since his marriage he had been writing literary and autobiographical articles for the newspapers. These were now collected and published under the title of *Chapter and Verse* (*Rede und Antwort*). The dedication was to the Faculty of Philosophy in the University of Bonn, of which he had recently been made a doctor *honoris causa*. The book appeared in 1922 and gave, in effect, an extremely lucid account rendered of the author's mental processes for some fifteen years past. The German people soon grew to know their Thomas Mann better than they knew any literary or even political figure of the epoch. Lectures, after-dinner speeches, letters, replies to various questionnaires and appeals, prefaces and introductions, painted a clear picture of a frank, generous but uncompromising spirit, provocative and progressive but founded firmly on the great traditions of the past in an age inconsistent to the verge of frivolity in its alternations of obscurantism and wild experiment.

But questions of direct policy were not touched on. Thomas Mann had nothing, at present, to add to the *Reflections* of 1918.

The eminence in these years of the versatile master, who united in his person so many literary and intellectual qualities generally divorced from one another, liberality of thought and respect for form, scepticism of mind and piety of heart, enthusiasm for life and sympathy with death, was enhanced by the publication in the same year, 1922, as *Chapter and Verse*, of a brilliant piece of purely imaginative literature which recalled the triumphs of pre-war days. This was the first instalment of *Felix Krull*, which had been written in 1910 and still awaited its sequel. The circumstances of the production of this work have been dealt with in an earlier chapter. In 1922 also appeared the first edition of the Collected Works, excluding *Buddenbrooks* and *Royal Highness*.

The former novel, which had now reached its majority, was still selling more steadily than any other book by Mann. How much its continued popularity owed to the huge success of a philosophical work which had been completed by a brilliant and profound critic of European society in 1914 and found a publisher in 1918, is doubtful. But Mann read with feelings appropriate to so subtle an ironist *The Decline of the West* by Oswald Spengler. In many respects this composition was a sociological comment on *Buddenbrooks*, which had preceded it in 1901. At any rate, no one, since Nietzsche, had propounded ideas more likely to interest the Thomas Mann who had changed, essentially, so little from the Thomas Mann of the turn of the century. He could not assent to Spengler's strict formulation of decadence into successive and mutually exclusive cycles of what appeared to him civilisations rather than cultures in the German sense. He found the sociology more French than German in conception, though he saw that the idea of cultural morphology had been borrowed from Goethe. Mann reprobated the materialism, the arbitrary view of natural process, the misconception, as he saw it, of the highest development of human nature, that he found in Spengler. Yet *The Decline of the West* necessarily stimulated, if only to repudiation of its formalism, the chronicler of the phenomenon of decadence in its private aspect and the analyst of cultural problems.

Certain notable evolutions along the general line of Mann's thought became evident as the second decade of the twentieth century proceeded. A study of the literary relation between Goethe and Tolstoy appeared in 1923. Those who remembered the theory of the psychology of the artist propounded in *Tonio Kröger* perceived that much water had flowed under the Mannian bridges during the last twenty years. The artist, for Goethe and Tolstoy were obviously artists, need no longer be necessarily a desperate outcast. The figure of Tonio Kröger was one-sided. Intuition was not, as a matter of course, one thing, and intelligence another. Such were some of the fundamental alterations, during this period, in the outlook of the author.

There were others, less stable and profound perhaps, but more conspicuous and more contradictory of certain previous opinions expressed by Mann. There were critics of the older school who even found that the author had shifted his ground reprehensibly. The *Reflections* of 1918, and especially the *Frederick the Great* of 1915, had been to a considerable extent apologetic, sober but emphatic, for a war of defence and liberation. *The German Republic*, an address printed in 1923 nominally for Gerhart Hauptmann on his sixtieth birthday but really for the republican youth of Germany, appeared to conservatives a recantation. It seemed to approve the *fait accompli*, the Heinrichian " progress," the Americanisation of the good old German god. But actually Thomas Mann had, with his usual abnormally acute vision, penetrated the gaudy exterior, the vulgar trappings of democracy, to its sound heart. The German revolution had, in fact, taught the teacher something. And he was the last man in the world to resist so positive an argument, even if it had to be enforced, to begin with, *ad hominem*. He knew that the democracy of the second decade of the century was not the dangerous and superficial brand of 1915. He had always known that the virtue of the soul of Germany did not depend upon military success. And he was prepared now to believe that intellectual merit has a better chance under popular government.

The German Republic reflects no more sinister phenomenon of Thomas Mann's mental experience than his developing Europeanism, which was already evident at the close of the war. His spirit was advancing beyond the German frontiers. But it was advancing, not, like the Heinrich Mann contingent, as light cavalry so mobile as to be dangerous to its own base, but with full and rich national equipment, with baggage complete to the last significant detail, like a migrant host.

In 1922-3 Mann had given lectures in Holland, Switzerland and Denmark. At the end of 1923 he visited Spain, where he preferred the severity of Castile to the exuberance of Andalusia, as was to be expected. He returned to Germany by sea, and touched at Plymouth for a few hours, his first sight of England. At home once more he devoted himself in the intervals of such experiences, including certain investigations into " occult " phenomena, as fall to the lot of eminent men of letters, to the final stages of a gigantic literary task. The novel upon which he had been engaged since 1912 was at last nearing completion.

CHAPTER V
FLORESCENCE

MANN was now in his fiftieth year. He had behind him a miscellaneous but largely imaginative literary output of an extraordinarily high and consistent level. A score of *Novellen*, two great novels, a play, a historical memoir, three volumes of essays and minor studies had already set him in the very front rank of European letters. He had the reputation of a writer who hardly ever sank below his best, who knew how to be original and progressive without making fantastic experiments. He was not a poet in the profound sense in which Hauptmann was. But he was that almost as rare bird, a teacher who was utterly serious without ever becoming tedious. His position was honourably eminent in the western world, he had no important enemies and his friends came from every class of society and every school of thought. There has seldom existed in literary history a figure so free from the least breath of any kind of detraction. Specimens of his work were being used in German schools as models of prose style. He was known to, corresponded with and visited literary men and literary societies all over Europe. In May 1924 he was the guest of honour at a dinner given by the P.E.N. Club in London and was welcomed from the Chair by John Galsworthy. The English translation of *Buddenbrooks* did not appear until the following September, so that people who did not read German only knew Mann as the author of *Royal Highness* and *Bashan and I*, which had been translated in 1916 and 1923 respectively. There was, however, an impression that *Buddenbrooks* could be compared with the Chairman's histories of the Forsytes. It was felt that the twin stars of the evening at Gatti's restaurant were well matched. The impression was erroneous in every respect except the details that both Mann and Galsworthy were concerned with recording the story of a family through more than one generation and that both were master craftsmen. The ideas and the styles governing the two conceptions were in fact altogether diverse. The parallel was not pursued at the dinner or subsequently. But Thomas Mann retained an admiring memory of the great English novelist. He turned it to account in a later article written to celebrate the sixtieth birthday of the author of *The Dark Flower*, which was the story preferred by the distinguished guest of 1924. Mr. and Mrs. H. G. Wells, Miss Violet Hunt and the late Stacy Aumonier were also present at the dinner. Galsworthy entertained Thomas Mann a day or two later at his house at Hendon, where the German novelist met Professor Gilbert Murray and the late William Archer. The language difficulty did not prevent mutual recognition during these encounters. It may be hoped that Mann's English visit will be repeated now that nearly ten years have elapsed and meanwhile the excellent and yearly increasing series of translations by Mrs. H. T. Lowe-Porter have been made available for readers in this country.

At the end of the year Messrs. Fischer published *The Magic Mountain*, a novel nearly three times the length of *Buddenbrooks*, which, twenty-five years before, they had wanted to cut down by half. They had learned profitable wisdom. The book was given a hundred impressions in four years and was at once translated into the principal European languages. An English version appeared in 1927. The scientific studies of Thomas Mann, including his examination of " psychic " phenomena, had mostly begun after the war, though he had been interested in disease since *Tristan*. These preoccupations found full and entertaining scope in the new masterpiece.

Only those whose songs are immortal, Oscar Wilde once said, should sing of death. Of Mann's title to immortality future generations will judge. The fact remains that death, almost as much as life, is the subject of *The Magic Mountain*, and that it is treated with every resource of the epic genius of the author. He had recently been in its presence. Julia Mann, *née* da Silva-Bruhn, had died peacefully, after a slight illness, in 1922. She is nowhere described, or even definitely suggested in Mann's literary work, though the mothers of his heroes are often of her gentle, somewhat exotic type. But her existence was capital to him as an artist and as a son. That " ardent and obscure impulse," which he attributed to the protagonist of *Death in Venice* as an inheritance from a mother who was the daughter of a Bohemian conductor of music, is hers. It had made him a writer in the first place. It is not impossible that the event of the elder Frau Mann's passage from life to death helped to deepen the spiritual significance of his latest *magnum opus*.

Thomas Mann's general experience of the years 1913-24, the war, politics, the revolution and the renewed influence of the thought of Goethe, is everywhere observable in *The Magic Mountain*. The figure of the austere young soldier, Joachim Ziemssen is one of the most striking and moving pieces of characterisation in the book : the debates between the brilliant humanist Settembrini and the sardonic Jesuit Naphta idealise the intellectual conflict of the times : the maturing of the spirit of the youthful principal, Hans Castorp, is a new perspective of the final nature of the sage of Weimar. The whole literal *Mountain* itself is conceived as the melting-pot of the essence of pre-war Europe, of that continent which was then still unconscious of what was happening to it and whose almost pathological state escaped the notice of all but a very few philosophical observers till four years of internecine struggle had laid bare for a grim analysis, as in the autopsy of a suicide by poison, the symptoms of a fatal corruption.

Not that Mann's analysis was at all portentously solemn. Experience could never, after his first youth, embitter him. The popularity of *The Magic Mountain* would not have been what it has come to be if that were the case. Irony and humour of first-class quality are as ubiquitous as ever in the new work. A great master in this style, Anatole France, was just dead. His mantle was worthily assumed by Thomas Mann, who is as lively and graceful, as solid and profound, as the great Frenchman and resembles France also in his dual position as a subtle artist acclaimed by the connoisseur and as a respected publicist who acts as pedagogue to simpler souls.

In June 1925 came Mann's fiftieth birthday and with it public recognition, documentary and otherwise, all over Germany, and not only in that country. The brilliant German author, journalist and critic, Arthur Eloesser, dedicated to him the study, *Thomas Mann, his Life and Work*, which in coloured and forcible prose epitomises a great man of letters. There were many other tributes, including the one hundred and fiftieth impression of *Buddenbrooks*. The notable events in Mann's life occur with cyclic regularity befitting his orderly genius. His first novel appears in 1900, twenty-five years after his birth, his marriage is celebrated in 1905, his fifty summers and a further *chef-d'œuvre* almost coincide twenty years later.

A new series of essays bearing a modest title which may almost be translated *Pains I Have Taken* or, less chattily, *Exertions*, appeared a few months after *The Magic Mountain*, and continued the effect of *Chapter and Verse*. In it he reprinted the greater part of *Goethe and Tolstoy* and also *The German Republic*. There was, too, a description of a pleasure cruise in the Mediterranean undertaken in the early part of 1925 which gave Mann his first actual physical contact with the East, though Athens "made him a European again." A defence of *The Magic Mountain* addressed to medical critics and some miscellaneous pieces completed the book.

In 1926 he was in Paris and shortly afterwards published the brief *Account of a Visit to Paris*, a diary of the nine January days he spent, accompanied by his wife, in the French capital. The apologist of German culture was deeply impressed by the cordiality of his reception. He gave a number of lectures, went to many parties, formal and informal, and met most of the more liberal of the French intellectuals, who seemed quite unabashed by the searching criticism of western democratic ideals which had been a feature of the *Reflections* of 1918. Henri Lichtenberger and Benjamin Crémieux were very amiable. Charles Du Bos compared the distinguished guest with Paul Valéry. Edmond Jaloux related the Lübeck of *Buddenbrooks* to the Marseilles of his own youth. Bertaux and the great Salomon Reinach talked of Oriental matters. Jules Romains and François Mauriac discussed Rolland and Galsworthy. Mereschovsky spoke of his novel dealing with Tut-ankh-amen and Mann was relieved to find that this book would not anticipate the sense of the work he was himself meditating. The French visit was a great success, too great, some cantankerous conservatives at home considered, and it was a valuable experience for the future development of a writer already a European and about to extend the range of his art to an even further horizon.

FLORESCENCE

A journey to Warsaw in 1927 completed Thomas Mann's round of inspection of the three principal enemies of Germany in the late war. He was everywhere enthusiastically received. There was no doubt that the best minds in Europe were sympathetic. Mann, without having ever consciously worked for such support, had received it in a measure which really astonished him. He had always found it a little mysterious that an artist should be honoured by society. He was not, indeed, the type of writer for whom public recognition is a necessity. But such recognition could not but be heartening and set him to work with renewed energy.

In the year 1926 had appeared the short story translated into English in 1929 under the title *Early Sorrow*, a greatly improved version of the central theme of the *Song about Childie*. There was, however, a further element in it, indicated by the German title which introduces the word " Disorder." The tale reflects incidentally, with Mann's accustomed penetration and humorous tolerance, the new " proletarian " society of the period of currency inflation in the Fatherland. It was a world as strange to him as to all his coevals and unlikely to commend itself to a fastidious artist. But by 1926 Thomas Mann was at home in the majority of all possible worlds. He did not satirise, he seemed hardly even to regret the brusque and careless manners, the mechanised minds, so much that appeared the coarsest and shallowest materialism in the rising generation. He merely recorded these contemporary characteristics and recorded, too, the

61

reactions to them of those in whom they were not native, dispensing to both sides the same suavely ironic pen and finding both equally amusing and instructive.

In the following year Julia, Thomas Mann's sole surviving sister, committed suicide, as Carla had seventeen years earlier. The circumstances are no business of a literary student unless they can be related to elements in his subject's literary performance. It is not possible, so far, to trace direct effects. No work of Mann since 1927 refers in any overt way to self-destruction, with the idea of which he had, all his life, even prior to 1910, been so familiar. The list of his imaginary suicides, from that of his very first hero, Friedemann, to Naphta's in *The Magic Mountain*, is a long one. But though there is murder in his last published story, *Mario and the Magician*, there is here no question of self-murder. The family tragedy of 1927 is noticed in the pages of the present work only for the sake of any possible bearing it may have on the estimate of any future literature by Mann. He has hinted that the story may contribute to a later narrative in an extensive setting, perhaps the great trilogy at present in progress.

For, some time in 1926 or 1927, a Munich artist had brought to Thomas Mann a portfolio of drawings illustrating the Old Testament tale of Joseph, the son of Jacob. The draughtsman had asked the eminent man of letters to write a preface to the publication of his designs. Mann referred, that evening, to his family Bible. What he read there started a train of thought destined to have important results. Goethe had admired the grace and point of the Hebrew fable and thought it capable of expansion into a piece of modern literature. Thomas Mann, meditating on the impulse which the contemporary interest in anthropology was giving to psychological research, agreed. To delve into the depths of past time, he reflected, was practically the same thing as to delve into the depths of the consciousness of man. What is earliest and oldest in humanity is likely to be also what is profoundest. The age that precedes the age of reason is also in a sense the stratum that underlies logical process in the mind. The myth that survives exhibits type more surely than any passing phase of the soul of man.

One could treat of these matters, he thought, in the way that Plato often did, rejecting superstition but not spirituality, rationalising but not vulgarising, with irony indeed, but without profanity. There was no sense in divorcing the legendary from psychological science. The establishment of a psychology of myth might be attempted by means taking account of the mythical element already implicit in the psychology of known behaviour.

Then there was the idea, which had always been present in the mind of a writer peculiarly conscious of his high destiny, of assimilating to one's art all that might be most significant in life and so contributing to the sum of human tradition and carrying it a further stage forward. Here was a significance that had so far been missed, even though Goethe may have had an inkling of it. The material itself had been used hundreds of times already by artists both in the western and in the oriental world. It was well known. And that made it all the more suitable for Mann's purpose. Everyone would know, at least, what he was talking about, and that would help them to see more readily what he was driving at. One has a far better chance of creating with familiar terms than with obscure elements.

Mann had read archaeology, as a boy, with more than childish curiosity. He had once confounded a schoolmaster, as he told Bertaux in Paris, by giving the correct native version of the Egyptian bull-god's name, Hapi, instead of the familiar graecised one, Apis. Gradually he conceived the idea of a trilogy, or triptych, on a historical-religious theme, of which one wing should deal with Joseph and his brothers, or, as came to seem more likely as the patriarchal figure loomed larger in his imagination, with Jacob and his sons, the other two with Spanish and German subjects. These latter, he conceived, were the countries in which the religious consciousness had reached fullest maturity in two different ways. After three thousand five hundred years some preliminary drafts of a new interpretation of the antique fable began to appear in two German literary periodicals. But a journey to the venerable sites of the legend became necessary. Thomas Mann departed, some three years after his interview with the painter, for the Near East.

The fourth lustre of the twentieth century drew to its close with a steady enhancement and ever wider dissemination of Mann's reputation. *Death in Venice,*

FLORESCENCE

Tristan and *Tonio Kröger* were translated into English in 1928. In the following year a signal honour was accorded to the author. He was summoned to Stockholm to receive the Nobel prize for literature. It was stated in the imposing document with which Mann was presented by King Gustav that the award was primarily due to the affection felt by the Scandinavian peoples for *Buddenbrooks*, that tale of a community settled by the northern sea. And, indeed, this work, with its nordic setting, rivalled the masterpieces of non-German Baltic lands in its homely ease, rich content and passages of austere eloquence. But there can be no question that if Mann had produced nothing else he would not have found himself in the select company of Anatole France, Rudyard Kipling, Sinclair Lewis and Gerhart Hauptmann. His name was not mentioned in connection with the prize until the year 1913, after the publication of *Death in Venice*, when *Fiorenza* and *Royal Highness*, too, had already added leaves to the laurel. Mann was therefore not unprepared for this event. But he describes its accompanying episodes, the festal progress to Sweden, the distinguished gatherings, the stately ceremonies, as the most impressive experience of his whole life.

Buddenbrooks he had written in the south, thinking of the north. A new *Novelle*, rather longer than *Death in Venice*, was now written by the Baltic coast, but dealt with an Italian subject. The action of *Mario and the Magician* takes place at a bathing resort on the Tyrrhenian Sea. The tale grew out of an original design to occupy the leisure of one summer holiday by noting down reminiscences of another in a warmer latitude. But the lightly begun commentaries took, finally, serious literary shape as a tragically imaginative story of cynical cruelty and desperate revenge. The melodrama is recognised for what it is. But the Italian setting, so appropriate to the theme, the old consummate realism and objectivity, the old skill of style and composition, make the tale completely successful. No winner of a Nobel prize could have done better.

Besides this *Novelle* Mann published in 1930 a new collection of lectures and articles dating between 1925 and 1929, under the title of *The Challenge of the Day* : a patriotic speech entitled *A German Address* and an auto-biographical *Sketch of my Life*. In 1932 appeared his Goethe centenary lecture, in which he laid stress on the great man's significance as a representative of that German burgher type which epitomises *Kultur*. It ended with the quotation in which the master calls for the rejection of worn-out machinery and the adoption, without reserve, of the new.

These are the latest published works of Thomas Mann. The story of his life experience so far as it affects his art reaches a temporary ending with his disappearance into Egypt and Palestine on the track of new beauty. The third decade of the century will witness the creation from that experience of a further monument, whose nature has not yet been clearly divulged, to enhance and adorn the complex and soaring structure of his genius.

PART II
THE CREATIVE ARTIST

CHAPTER I
THE IDEA OF DECADENCE

THOMAS MANN'S first volume was published in 1898, when he was twenty-three years old. But he had been recognised as a writer, in the sense of having had his work printed, since he was nineteen. Most of the six *Novellen* which made up the volume of '98 had already appeared in periodicals, and there were also certain minor contributions, principally in verse, which were not re-issued.

His name was therefore not altogether unknown, and it already stood for a distinct literary personality. For Mann, like the earliest European patroness of literature, had sprung fully armed into the world of words. The difference between the new author and a hundred other contemporary young fellow-craftsmen of a romantic and melancholy turn of mind was that Mann already showed the detachment and the careful ingenuity of the born artist. Where others fitfully raged and dreamed he continuously chronicled and examined. But a real, if un-sentimental, human sympathy lay behind the catalogue of fastidiously chosen detail and the piercing, ironic analysis. The stories, coolly presented as they were, stimulated the emotions as effectively as they did the intellect.

And that was more than could be said of the majority of the fashionable imitators of Zola, Huysmans and the new French school of impressionism.

The six narratives contained in this first book, which was entitled, like the opening tale, *Little Herr Friedemann*, dealt, as all fiction that is meant for an adult public must deal, with psychological conflict. They were all studies in dissension, the dissension between what is familiar and what is strange. This phenomenon seemed to Mann the most conspicuous element in what he saw when he looked out upon the world and when he looked into his own heart. On the one hand he perceived, for example, the normal citizen, confident, active, sensible, unimaginative, *l'homme moyen sensuel*. On the other side moved uncertainly the dim figure of the exception, the outlaw, critical, passive, unstable, a prey to odd fancies and visions beyond the veil of matter.

The clash, it seemed to Thomas Mann at this period, whether it occurs between separate personalities or in a single individual, is bound to produce unhappiness. At best the result, in life or in literature, will be an elegy, at worst a tragedy. These six stories are all either one or the other. The interest is in each case focussed on the peculiar character, the misfit, who feels himself a stranger in a strange land. The mere fact that he is in a very small minority seems to indicate that he is more than a variation from type: he is a declension from his kind, a decadent. And he is conscious of it, as he must be if he enters human society at all. His reaction may be revolt or despair, in proportion to his strength or his weakness. But in either case he naturally and instinctively hates the majority, while still more or less subconsciously regretting that he is not of them, as Catullus hated Lesbia while he loved her. The bitter epigram of the Roman poet might have been placed as a motto to the volume entitled *Little Herr Friedemann.**

The title story gives perhaps the best and fullest treatment of this idea. Johann Friedemann is a hunchback— Thomas Mann has a pronounced taste for corporal peculiarities—and generally of poor physique. But his intelligence and his will-power, as not infrequently occurs in cases of physical eccentricity, are above the average. There is scarcely a hint, certainly no example, throughout Mann's work of the Greek ideal of the philosopher-athlete. The notion of an ingenious mind is for him practically inseparable from that of an ineffectual body, a complex of relations binding these two concepts into a system which at times, in him, becomes a theory. Johann's hump excludes him from any unalloyed pleasure in society, though he takes a part in the commercial and intellectual life of his native town. He consciously makes his existence as purely mental as he can. He is an amateur of the theatre and finds himself, one evening, seated next to a woman of striking beauty, Frau von Rinnlingen, in whose features, however, are evident certain traces of cunning and brutality. Her eyes are too

---

* *Odi et amo.   Quare id faciam fortasse requiris.*
  Nescio, sed fieri sentio et excrucior.   Cat. *Carm.* lxxxv.

close together and her under-lip projects, like Nero's. Friedemann's sisters call on her, and after some hesitation he follows them. She invites him to a party. During this function they stroll together, at her suggestion, in the moonlit garden, and find a secluded seat by the river. Friedemann is unable to conceal his passion, which her apparent sympathy had encouraged. She rejects his advances with the merciless cruelty of a child or an animal. The case is hopeless. To Friedemann it proves his ineradicable decadence. With cool restraint the author depicts the suicide by drowning of his courageous and gifted hero, defeated by the coarse materialism of Frau von Rinnlingen, of life in the raw, the life he sub-consciously loved and wished to share. The leisurely detail, the vivid characterisation, the swift, natural and dramatic dialogue, the sharp irony that does not spare even the unhappy principal himself, are all astonishingly mature in this brief but poignant study. *Little Herr Friedemann* is the evident bud of the genius that was to flower miraculously during the next thirty years.

The second most important tale in this collection is called *Der Bajazzo*, the Italian word for trickster or mountebank. It is more elegiac in tone and treatment than the first. The protagonist is too weak to be a hero of tragedy. As a boy he had been nicknamed " Bajazzo " by an unsympathetic father whose nordic temperament could only endure to use the soft Italian tongue in scorn. The portrait of this gentleman exhibits certain traces, mostly external, the decisive, elegant manners, the

shrewd, cool speech, of the character of Mann's own
progenitor. It is obvious that the tale dates from the
Roman sojourn of the author, which threw into relief,
for him, the contrast between Latin and Teutonic types.
There is far less dialogue and drama than in the tragic
Friedemann. The story is a confession, told in the first
person ; in certain directions, perhaps, it is an autobio-
graphy, though in any case less of Thomas than of his
brother Heinrich. At all events the " Bajazzo " was a
rather more showy young man than Thomas in his
adolescence. But he is a jack of all trades and master of
none, is a spectator only, has no creative ability. The
character resembles far more closely than Friedemann
the popular idea of what constitutes human decadence.
The boy, whose childhood has been relatively happy—
the mother was more sympathetic than the father—becomes financially independent on the death of his parents.
He cultivates the garden of Epicurus, but finds that selfish enjoyment, even of art and literature, brings only
boredom. The didactic note here, as rarely in Mann, is
marked and explicit. The sermon treads closely on the
heels of the confession. Ashamed of his useless and misdirected life the " Bajazzo " throws himself at the feet of
Anna Rainer, the moderately intelligent, healthy and
prosaically attractive girl, who naturally rejects him to
become the wife of a man of her own type.

The pictures of the shy, sensitive young *rentier*, lonely
and wretched behind the pleasant-seeming outward circumstances of financial independence ; of the aesthete,

awkward and bored in society, morbidly introspective out of it, have all the biting realism that was to make *Buddenbrooks* famous. Neither Flaubert nor Huysmans, whose atmospheres this story often recalls, surpass at their best the twenty-five-year-old Mann in this literary quality, which fixes permanently and poignantly in the mind scenes and ideas already perfectly familiar to the reader. The only real passion of the " Bajazzo " is envy of the *Lichtmenschen*, the children of light, those happy, simple people who are never at a loss, to whom life is always kind, because they are her own, the sun's kindred. " I am bound to hate them," murmurs the sad epicurean, " but my hate is nothing but poisoned love."

The story has no climax. The betrothal of Anna Rainer to the excellent Dr. Witznagel, which was a foregone conclusion, is announced. The " Bajazzo " turns back, with a last hopeless sigh, to the life that mocks him as he used to mock the masters when he was at school.

Tobias Mindernickel, a third narrative, is also striking for its deeply and darkly etched portrait of a worthless, though not positively wicked personality. The name implies a value of less than a piece of the nickel coinage still current in Germany. Mann, like Shakespeare, Dickens and the Goncourts, has a fondness for names that have a direct revealing value for character. Mindernickel is a shy, feeble and shabby individual, originally an altruist and prepared to love his enemies. But " his face looked as though life, uttering a scornful laugh, had struck it with a heavily clenched fist." His walk was like that of "a man hastening through a sudden down-pour without an umbrella." Nietzsche would have hunted him triumphantly to ruin. But society, except that proportion of it which consists of rude little boys, merely ignores a creature so contemptible and degenerate that he continually gets on the nerves even of the most cynical reader.

Yet, with all this, Mindernickel is still capable of Nietzschean will to power. When one of the children pursuing him falls down and bursts out crying the butt of the neighbourhood returns to bind up the scratch and walks off at last with great pride amidst the awe of his former tormentors. Next day, however, the usual juvenile hue and cry begins again.

Then the most lonely and despised of men purchases a dog, less for the purpose of acquiring its companionship and affection than to possess some living thing which will defer to him. He wants to experience the, to him, utterly unknown sensations of a master. He succeeds in making this insignificant animal obey him for a time. But when the dog is tired it naturally refuses to answer to the name he has given it. Mindernickel flies into a passion. "I tell you, you must come, even when you ARE tired," he cries angrily, and beats the small creature with vicious cruelty. Then, while it lies whining on the floor, he strides up and down with the mien of a victorious hero. He pauses to address the animal in the cold, ironical phrase used by Napoleon to the regiment that had con-trived to lose its eagle during a battle. "May I ask how you came to behave like this ? " The dog slinks, whimpering, to his feet. In a paroxysm of magnanimity he seizes and embraces it, tears in his eyes.

Another day, he is feeding his pet with a knife, when it makes a clumsy spring and gets the blade stuck in its shoulder. The embittered altruist, hungry still for domination, is delighted to have the opportunity, a third time, of showing generous tenderness. He is quite sorry when, some days later, the dog is cured in consequence of his ministrations. However, he takes it in his arms, as usual, to fondle it. But the little animal is now feeling more lively, and jumps away from him. Mindernickel's blind rage flares up again. He catches hold of the feeding-knife and drives it into the newly healed wound. This time, in spite of his master's contrite attentions, the dog dies.

Such a theme would suggest in another writer satire carried to the limits of ferocity and caricature. But the art of Thomas Mann, far ahead of its time in the psychological insight shown, leaves the reader moved and compassionate, prepared, even if he be as enthusiastic a lover of dogs as Mann himself already then was, to feel that the wretched Tobias Mindernickel was more sinned against than sinning.

More strictly a story, less, that is, of a sketch, an elegy, is that of the painter Paolo Hofmann, born, like Mann himself, of a South American mother. The name, with its Italo-Germanic ring, is also significant. The tale is entitled *The Will to Happiness*. Hofmann is mortally diseased, his heart is weak, but his iron will keeps him alive for five years, until the father of the girl he loves has given his consent to their marriage. The refusal was due to the parent's suspicion of Hofmann's disability, but the girl, a voluptuous, half Jewish beauty, loves him. On the morning after the wedding night the artist is found dead. He, the exception, the outcast, has succeeded in uniting himself with the normal. But it has killed him. Or rather, perhaps, there was nothing more to keep him alive, once his desire had been fulfilled. The familiar, at any rate, as in the other tales, has overwhelmed the strange, though less easily than usual.

The story is supposed to be told by a friend of the painter's, who meets him in Rome, five years after the first meeting with the girl, which took place in Munich. The teller of the tale gives Hofmann the welcome message with which he has been entrusted by the parents, and sees a strange expression on the artist's yellow face, " the fierce, convulsively strained immobility of a beast of prey about to spring." This changes, when the lover leaves Rome to go to his wedding, to a look of grave triumph, which his friend observes later, at the funeral, on the countenance of the widow. The narrative is fundamentally a study of the potentialities of the human will.

The two remaining stories in this collection are slighter in content. *Disappointment* is the lament of a megalomaniac. The narrator is buttonholed by a lugubrious stranger in St. Mark's Square at Venice and forced to listen to his woes. The fellow looks like an Englishman, might be any age between thirty and fifty. He has an enigmatic and rather silly smile. It appears that he has gathered from his education a pathetic faith in such abstractions as good and evil, beauty and ugliness. He expected great things of life, terrible and delightful. But he is continually compelled to ask, "Is that all?" Pleasure and pain, luck and misfortune, even the fire that burnt down his parents' house, all disappoint him.

This, like *Der Bajazzo*, is a tale of the confessional, autobiographical type. The stranger cannot even find anything to admire in the fantastic loveliness of the scene around him. He is actually certain that death itself, when it comes to him, will be disappointingly banal. Even Schopenhauer, who has presided over the story so far, could not have reached so bizarre a conclusion. The moral is evident. Reality disappoints only those too poorly equipped to contribute to it. The world's desire and expectation of us is more than our desire and expectation of the world. The irresolute are always hypercritical, weary and stale, like Hamlet. The wretched stranger, Mann hints, is improperly resigned to, even enjoys, his excessive yearnings, and so is doomed.

Death is a further study of life-weariness, carried to a detailed analysis that verges on monotony. It is distinctly the weakest of the six tales and has never been reprinted.

Three of these stories, *Little Herr Friedemann*, *Der Bajazzo* and *Tobias Mindernickel* may reasonably be regarded as preliminary exercises to the great masterpiece which appeared in 1901. The physical weakness of the central figures, the courage of Friedemann, the gaudiness of Bajazzo, the shy, hypersensitiveness of Mindernickel were to re-appear in three of the principal characters of *Buddenbrooks*, actually in three of the members of that ancient and honourable house. Ideas such as that of the raw, blunt cruelty of life, the unsuitability of the volatile artistic temperament for the solid business of practical living and the self-torture that results from the attempt to conquer the feeling of being a square peg in a round hole, the whole notion of decadence as a frailty, a declension from sanity, and yet mysteriously seductive in its appeal to pity and the sense of wonder, enter into the first long novel by Thomas Mann.

His readers knew more or less what to expect and they found it. But they found it in a richly varied and vast, an epic atmosphere, one too, since it was entirely commercial, that the rather exclusively " bohemian " setting of most of the preceding stories would seem to have forbidden to the author. There was as much astonishment as admiration in the first wave of enthusiasm for *Buddenbrooks*.

The novel opens in the year 1835. Johann Buddenbrook, head of the wealthy firm of grain merchants founded by his ancestor in 1768, is a genial old materialist, an admirer of Voltaire and Napoleon, a sceptical, cool, hard-headed business man through and through. His friends and contemporaries are the humorous, worldly *abbé*, Pastor Wunderlich, and the rococo, typically eighteenth-century poet Hoffstede, who writes a charming trifle to celebrate the house-warming party given by the Buddenbrook family and brilliantly described in the first thirty pages of the book. The three generations which are to exemplify the idea of decadence implicit in the sub-title of the novel, *Decline of a Family*, are already present on this occasion. Johann, son of old Buddenbrook, is a mature benedict, serious-minded and inclined to piety, though still not far inferior to his father as a business man. His ideal, at which old Johann good-humouredly scoffs, is the age's notion of progress as incarnated in the contemporary king of France, Louis Philippe. The younger Johann's three small children, Thomas, Antonie and Christian, already show certain further divergences from the family type. In the first two generations the contrast between the gay and somewhat cynical, Frenchified elders, old Johann and his friends, and the more solemn and sentimental epoch which was succeeding Goethe and the romantics is very noticeable to a reader who may have been accustomed in his youth to adolescent scepticism and parental austerity. Of the children it is the seven-year-old Christian, with his nervous excitability, who is, at the moment, chiefly significant. Or perhaps a better word would be, ominous.

From this point until the sudden death in 1855 of the younger Johann Buddenbrook, who is still only on the threshold of old age—his father predeceases him by many years—the reader feels himself to be in a world definitely

of the past. The characters, the settings, the conversational idioms, the clothes, the history itself of the period,
including the revolutionary tumults of 1848, are amaz-
ingly vivid and delineated with the accuracy and consis-
tency which are conspicuous features of all Thomas
Mann's work. He had his own family archives to draw
upon. The Buddenbrooks, who resemble very closely the
ancestors of Mann himself, had theirs too. But the historical imagination, as he was to show again and again in
future years, is a peculiar gift in his versatile psychology.

With the accession of the young Thomas Buddenbrook to the headship of the firm the Wagnerian over-
ture, containing the fundamental *motifs* of what is to
follow, concludes. The development of the main theme
of decadence now gathers force and complexity. Thomas
Buddenbrook, though he occupies considerably less
space in the novel as a whole than his enchanting sister
Toni, sustains the most serious burden of commentary.
Like Johann Friedemann and Paolo Hofmann he is a true
tragic hero in the German sense of a strong man whose
strength is nevertheless not equal to his fate. He is
efficient in commerce, but he is the first Buddenbrook
for whom to be efficient in commerce is to make an effort.
His mind takes account of other things besides buying
cheap and selling dear. Like Mann's own father he has
certain literary, even, just before his death, philosophical,
interests. And he marries, as Johann Mann did, a
mysterious beauty whose soul is in her music. He is the
first " individual " in the firm, but he pays heavily for

setting his personality against the mass-consciousness of his time. Physically he is not strong. For the last few years, especially, of his comparatively brief life he suffers from nerves, not improved by the eternal cigarettes which are a characteristic resource of the age. *Il faut toujours avoir une cigarette*, maintains a famous French decadent * only a few years later than this period, at the beginning of one of his best known satirical tales. Thomas Buddenbrook is also a victim of high blood-pressure and the life-weariness which Mann had already noted in his *Novellen* as one of the definitive symptoms of decadence.

A celebrated passage at the end of a chapter preluding this hero's end marks the final stage of the elegant and efficient merchant's conflict with his fate. He is standing, with his sister Toni, on a desolate seashore.

" ' Great waves,' said Thomas Buddenbrook. ' How they come on and break, come on and break, one after another, endlessly, idly, empty and vast ! And yet, like all the simple, inevitable things, they soothe, they console, after all. I have learned to love the sea more and more. Once, I think, I cared more for the mountains, because they lay farther off. Now I do not long for them. They would only frighten and abash me. They are too capricious, too manifold, too anomalous. I know I should feel myself vanquished in their presence. What sort of men prefer the monotony of the sea ? Those, I think, who have looked so long and deeply into the

* Pierre Louÿs.

little grains of sand were sticking. At the very bottom, in Papa's small, neat handwriting, that ran so fast over the page, he read his own name under that of his parents, Justus Johann Kaspar, born April 15, 1861. He liked looking at it. He straightened up a little and took the ruler and pen, still rather idly, let his eye travel once more over the whole genealogical host, then with absent care, mechanically and dreamily, he made with the gold pen a beautiful, clean, double line diagonally across the entire page, the upper one heavier than the lower, just as he had been taught to embellish the page of his arith- metic book. He looked at his work with his head on one side and then moved away.

After dinner the Senator called him up and surveyed him with his eyebrows drawn together.

'What is this? Where did it come from? Did you do it?'

Hanno had to think a minute whether he really had done it. Then he answered:

'Yes.'

'What for? What is the matter with you? Answer me! What possessed you to do such a mischievous thing?' cried the Senator, and struck Hanno's cheek lightly with the rolled up notebook.

And little Johann stammered, retreating with his hands to his cheek:

'I thought—I thought—there was nothing else coming.'" *

* Translation by H. T. Lowe-Porter

Soon after Thomas Buddenbrook's fatal stroke his child dies of typhus. For life is will, according to Schopenhauer, and Hanno has not inherited his father's strength of character. The old house is bought by a rising Jewish family, the Buddenbrooks are dispersed. Only the invincible Toni survives. The resolution of the theme, the third movement of the symphony, ends in a fugal lament for the cruel war of destruction waged by life.

This novel is epic in scale, conception and treatment. It grew to its extensive, but not excessive, proportions out of Mann's own experience in early youth, which led him to account for the financial misfortunes of his own family by a reference to the gradual outcropping of non-commercial instincts, becoming definitely of an artistic type in himself, his brother and younger sister. Hence arose the idea of an artist as a decadent, one who refuses to accept the normal life of a specifically commercial age and who is therefore an outcast, a useless declension from type. Christian Buddenbrook with his sensitiveness amounting in the eyes of the sober citizen to mania, his restive recusancy of a decent, stable existence, his mimetic talent blocked by his extreme nervousness, his utter lack of reserve, is the first clear example in the house of Buddenbrook, as perhaps Heinrich Mann had been in the author's own, of the indubitably artistic temperament. The portrait is a bitter caricature which fails to be cruel only because of the typical sympathetic irony which informs it. The reader ends by pitying as much as he despises Christian the mountebank, the charlatan, the weak debauchee and hypochondriac. Thomas Buddenbrook's thunderous scorn in the great scene between the brothers after their mother's death is almost counterbalanced by the shrill Strindbergian protest of the culprit.

" ' Don't you realise, you fool,' cried Thomas Buddenbrook in a passion, ' that all these horrors are the consequence and effect of your vices, your idleness and your self-tormenting? Go to work! Stop petting your condition and talking about it !' . . . ' Work! Suppose I can't work? My God! I can't do the same thing long at a time! It kills me. If you have been able to and are able to, thank God for it, but don't sit in judgment on others, for it isn't a virtue. God gives strength to one and not to another. But that is the way you are made, Thomas. You are self-righteous. Oh, wait, that is not what I am going to say, nor what I accuse you of. I don't know where to begin and however much I can say is only a millionth part of the feeling I have in my heart against you. You have made a position for yourself in life and there you stand and push everything away which might possibly disturb your equilibrium for a moment— for your equilibrium is the most precious thing in the world to you. But it isn't the most precious thing in life, Thomas—no, before God it is not. You are an egoist, that is what you are. I am still fond of you, even when you are angry and tread on me and thunder me down. But when you get silent, when somebody says something and you are suddenly dumb and withdraw yourself, quite elegant and remote, and repulse people like a wall and leave the other fellow to his shame without any chance of justifying himself— ! Yes, you are without pity, without love, without humility. Oh,' he cried, and stretched both arms in front of him, palms outward, as though pushing everything away from him, ' Oh, how sick I am of all this tact and propriety, this poise and refinement—sick to death of it ! '

The outburst was so genuine, so heartfelt, it sounded so full of loathing and satiety that it was actually crushing. Thomas shrank a little and looked down in front of him, weary and without a word." *

Each voice is that of Thomas Mann. And their conflict is the storm that ploughed the virgin fields of his youth and made them bear the first harvest, in *Buddenbrooks*, of his greatness.

The young writer had discovered at school that his originally vague notions of the ruinous antithesis between burgher and artist, between the robust business man and the delicate intellectual, had been anticipated by Friedrich Nietzsche. That philosopher's sweeping and vindictive analysis of decadence had cleared his conceptions. But Thomas Mann had a level head. He suspended judgment, merely chronicled, with a greater elaboration and a cooler insight, the workings of the struggle. The end of *Buddenbrooks* is no vindication of either side. It leaves the reader with a sense as much of the admirable vitality

* Translation by H. T. Lowe-Porter.

of the unimaginative merchant as of his ruthlessness, with a sense as much of the marvellous intuition of the aesthetic temper as of its futile cowardice.

This drawn battle is waged with every resource of epic genius. Its movement is in the depths of thought and feeling, its picture is the vivid and accurate reflection of the world in the soul of a single personality, its technique is as polished, as ingenious and as effective as that of Homer. Thomas Mann, in the nursery, had preferred Hector and Achilles to Hawkeye and Leatherstocking. The *Leitmotiv*, the device invented by the author of the Iliad and patented by Wagner, is a prominent feature of the style of *Buddenbrooks*. The autocrat of Bayreuth had early become an influence scarcely inferior to that of his friend and subsequent enemy Nietzsche in the life of the young amateur, for whom music was so much more than a pendant to literature. The contrivance was not new to letters. Besides Homer the modern Europeans Goethe, Zola and Dickens, to name only three of many writers, had used it. But Mann was a musician and his repetitive notes have a value not only intellectual but emotional. Thomas Buddenbrook's trick of raising one eyebrow draws attention, when it is referred to, as much to the significant mood of a passage as to its logical importance in the development of the plot. When poor Toni unconsciously quotes, as she does at intervals throughout her long life, the phrases used by the revolutionary young doctor, who was the object of her early, unhappy and only love, the deft and unobtrusive hint thus introduced into the narrative deepens almost intolerably the tragedy of her life and through her tragedy the tragedy of her house. Not Wagner himself equals Thomas Mann's dexterous mastery of such effects, which can be, as they not infrequently are in the composer, deprived of value by over-emphasis, incongruous appearance and excessive repetition, tending to become mechanical and at last empty.

Wagner's works have been called the artistic interpretation of the philosophy of Schopenhauer, whose view of and deep interest in music explains so much of his general theory. It is true that the pages in the operatic scores devoted to the fateful figures of Wotan and Tristan seem to support this contention. But, however this may be, it is clear that of the spiritual sponsors of *Buddenbrooks* the third great intellect, apart from Nietzsche, in whose work, too, music looms large, and Wagner, is the apologist of pessimism. He is only mentioned explicitly when Thomas Buddenbrook is near his end. The outwardly imperturbable, inwardly stricken and weary head of the ancient house finds an incomplete copy of *The World as Will and Idea* in a summer pavilion of the new and elegant mansion for which, since his marriage, he has deserted—another symptom of decadence—the venerable pile occupied by his forefathers.

" He was filled with a great, surpassing satisfaction. It soothed him to see how a master mind could lay hold on the strong, cruel, mocking thing called life, dominate it and condemn it. His was the gratification of the sufferer

who has always had a bad conscience about his sufferings
and conceals them from the gaze of a harsh, unsympathetic world until suddenly, from the hand of an
authority, he receives, as it were, justification and licence
for his suffering, justification before the world, this best
of all possible worlds, which the master-mind scornfully
demonstrates to be the worst of all possible ones." *

Schopenhauer, with his peculiar doctrine of personal
immortality, prepares Thomas Buddenbrook for death.
But, with Nietzsche, the earlier philosopher is behind the
whole conception of the idea of decadence in the novel.
At the third stage, where the focus of the treatment is
the little Hanno, Wagner takes over. For Hanno, to
understand *Tristan und Isolde* is to die. His improvisa-
tion on the piano in the last chapter but two of *Buddenbrooks*, just before he is taken ill with typhus, is Wagnerian. It is the composition of a child. But throughout
the brilliant description of it, which occupies three full
pages in the book, the tragic pathos of the life of a man
is marvellously conveyed.

" The fanatical worship of this worthless trifle, this
scrap of melody, this brief, childish harmonic invention,
only a bar and a half in length, had about it something
stupid and gross and at the same time something ascetic
and religious, something that contained the essence of
faith and renunciation. There was a quality of the perverse in the insatiability with which it was produced and
revelled in : there was a sort of cynical despair, there was

* Translation by H. T. Lowe-Porter.

a longing for joy, a yielding to desire, in the way the last drop of sweetness was, as it were, extracted from the melody till exhaustion, disgust and satiety supervened. Then at last, at last, in the weariness after excess a long, soft arpeggio in the minor trickled through, mounted a tone, resolved itself in the major and died in mournful lingering away.

Hanno sat still a moment, his chin on his breast, his hands in his lap. Then he got up and closed the instrument. He was very pale, there was no strength in his knees and his eyes were burning. He went into the next room, stretched himself on the *chaise-longue* and remained for a long time motionless." *

The main presentation of the idea of decadence in *Buddenbrooks*, the gradually darkening picture of the decline of a great trading family through increasing sensibility, is enhanced by a hundred subordinate touches throwing the variants of character and atmosphere into a relief that not only prevents the tragedy from becoming intolerable but lifts it into the air of the highest comedy.

It is Toni Buddenbrook, that Madame Bovary seen through German spectacles, an eight-year-old child on the first page of the book, a woman of fifty with the face and the nature of a child on its last, who softens the stark outlines, warms the sharp air of this narrative of inexorable destiny. All Germany and, as time went on, most of Europe, fell in love with her. Her quaint docility, her instant and intense, if brief, reactions to

* Translation by H. T. Lowe-Porter.

pleasures and pains, her absurd and fascinating dignity, her dauntless vitality, revive a complex feminine charm that, in its entirety, has vanished with the " emancipation " of the sex.

An episode very typical of life in the forties of the last century establishes Toni, at eighteen or so, once for all as a tragic figure in the book. Her character appears to remain unchanged. But it is this very fact which increases the emotional tension. Toni does not need any more to draw in her chin and raise her shoulders, in that delightful way of hers, at important moments, though she continues to do so. She has henceforth in the reader's mind the melancholy majesty of a princess of Sophocles beneath her lively, infantile envelope, however incontestably a part of herself that envelope persists. It is significant that her most dramatic gesture, to pass her tongue over her upper lip, is a prelude sometimes to laughter and sometimes to tears.

Herr Bendix Grünlich was a pretty young gentleman with a rosy face, long golden whiskers and a feebly criminal mentality. He imposed on the upright and industrious man of business, Johann Buddenbrook the Second, but not on the innocent Toni, who hated him at sight. Her father took the traditional view. The *partie*, he considered, was an advantageous one. His daughter was too young to know her own mind. She must go to the seaside to think it over. Toni went, and met Morten Schwarzkopf, the medical student who was anticipating the theories of Garibaldi. The idyll by the northern sea, which Mann knew and loved so intimately, has an ethereal sweetness and poignancy. But it is crowned only by a single kiss. Grünlich appears, Morten's father intervenes, Toni returns, family feeling crushes natural instinct. The first of the ominous marriages of convenience takes place, with the inevitable result. Johann had to fetch his daughter home and the union was dissolved.

In spite of this affair and the equally disastrous second marriage with a grossly festive and unbalanced, not to say unbuttoned, Bavarian—a further variety of decadent —Toni continues to provide quite half the humour in a novel singularly rich in that quality. Her very agonies, as so often happens in life, exhibit the comic strain. The telegram in which she announces her second matrimonial failure is an admirably ironic epitome of her nature, with its contrasting touches of imperiousness and self-dramatisation.

"'Don't be frightened. Am coming at once with Erica. All is over. Your unhappy Antonie.'"

Again, at Thomas Buddenbrook's death-bed, in the presence of the whole grief-stricken family, Toni began to sing a hymn in a loud voice, but found she could only remember the first three lines " and had to make up for her abrupt ending by the increased dignity of her manner."

Buddenbrooks, perhaps more than any other European novel published before 1900, certainly more than any other German novel, conveys convincingly the sense of what Rabelais called life itself, "*ceste insigne fable et tragicque comédie.*"

The secondary ideas and influences at work in the book were not often new to those who had read *Little Herr Friedemann* carefully. They were in general consistent with the literary personality with which the earlier production had already invested Thomas Mann. It is the epic note, the sway of Tolstoy, and the consequent elaboration of the thought, which chiefly differentiate *Buddenbrooks* from the *Novellen*. Music had taught Mann to compose, like Homer and Milton, a logical texture woven of different themes and this method incalculably enriched his style and form. He was not by any means exclusively devoted to Wagnerism, which has certain decadent aspects only appropriate when the main theme of the novel is in full play. Bach, and more particularly Chopin, preside in many passages. The fastidious elegance, however, of the writing, throughout the book, never otherwise than fit for an aristocratic *salon*, has always the sureness and the continuous charm of the Polish composer, his extreme intelligence and avoidance of the commonplace, his extraordinary faculty for translating the most tragic and profound desires of the soul into polite language. So, too, the exact framework, the use of counterpoint, climax and, in the more crowded scenes, of chorus, recall the idiom of Bach, as do the rhythmic rise and fall of mood, the storms and the breezes of the style, the touches of humour, the symbolic phrases, the more or less elusive hints and suggestions.

Like a musician, again, Mann respects his material, knows the souls of words, understands their potential melody, their dynamic power.

The texture of the prose, in fact, as that of a good symphony should be, is so closely studied, the intellectual analysis so concentrated, all facile thought, feeling and expression so rigorously pruned, that it is easy to remember how *Buddenbrooks* was written. It was composed as in a laboratory, behind the closed doors of the flat in Rome, shut in the narrow rooms at Munich, while an alien life streamed by unmarked, without significance for the slowly growing pile of manuscript.

Lübeck only was near, and the grey Baltic, whose air swept through the Scandinavian romances read in the Via Torre Argentina. Such dream-images were clearer in the author's mind than those of the two southern cities where his novel was conceived and executed. They make the pictures in *Buddenbrooks*, the interiors, the streets, the land and sea-scapes, the West Prussian bodies and minds. They make the thought acute and tender, the style pure and flexible, of a masterpiece that stands alone in German literature.

In the year 1903 Thomas Mann published a further collection of *Novellen* under the general title of *Tristan*. He was, as the quotation from Ibsen which prefaced the text indicated, going to law with himself. The stories carry the analysis of the idea of decadence to a new stage. The inner dissension appears as still more malignant, because the personal note is less disguised, than in

Buddenbrooks. The critics, especially those under thirty, hesitated no longer. Thomas Mann was indubitably a great writer. Some even affirmed that he was greater than the mighty figure whose outlines could still be discerned in this third volume, Friedrich Nietzsche.

Of the six tales *Tonio Kröger* is by far the most important. It is the *locus classicus* for the ideas that governed Thomas Mann's mind between 1900 and 1905, and for many that remain with him still. And it is also, technically, a choice example of the realistic-romantic idiom which the author had long made peculiarly his own. Its rich but melancholy cadences, that were yet so crystal clear and sharp to the taste with their restrained irony, resemble nothing so much as one of those rare and delicate wines that educate and enhance, rather than merely excite, the qualities of mind and heart that deserve them. The younger members of Mann's audience, in particular, were permanently enthralled by *Tonio Kröger*. A student at Göttingen long afterwards told the author, when he was lecturing at that university, that this tale was his most characteristic work. It has, at any rate, always been a favourite piece for its creator.

The plot hardly exists in any strict sense. Kröger, at fourteen, admires his schoolfellow, the handsome, athletic and industrious Hans Hansen, as Thomas Mann had admired a similar figure at his own school. As an adolescent Kröger loves the cheerful, pretty and healthy Ingeborg Holm. But neither she nor Hans take him seriously. He goes to Italy and lectures his friend, the woman

G   97

THOMAS MANN

painter Lisaweta Ivanovna, on art and artists. He returns, after thirteen years, now an established writer, to his native town, where he is nearly arrested, as Mann had nearly been on a similar occasion, in mistake for a criminal. He sees again, in Denmark, Hans and Ingeborg, or their types, and writes his conclusions to Lisaweta.

This tale is significantly dedicated to Kurt Martens, one of Mann's Munich friends, who had in vain besought him to " live." But the artist, says Kröger, cannot afford to live, if to live is to feel like other people. Nor can the man who lives and feels normally become an artist. It is one thing or the other. Hans will never read Schiller's *Don Carlos*, nor write verses. Yet Kröger longs to make Hans his friend and Ingeborg his lover. He seeks painfully, as Schiller said the poet should, that " nature " or truth, which comes so easily to the simple, as to the frank, intuitive, unselfconscious mind of a Goethe or a Hauptmann. But he is unsuccessful. Not in his works, which are acclaimed, but in his days.

Tonio Kröger is not quite a tragedy. The hero, for he is one, a fighter, a self-masterer as well as a self-tormentor, lives on. But life has defeated him, as it defeated Goethe's Tasso, who wished to throw away his lyre and draw the sword. And he has not Tasso's consolation. For he does not believe in his genius, or in any man's. Genius is useless, not regenerative, but degenerate. The " naive " only, the " bourgeois," are useful and productive. Tonio Kröger will never be happy, because he is at heart a " bourgeois " strayed from the narrow path,

98

an artist, as he calls himself, with a " bad conscience."
He is ashamed of himself, and shame makes him moralise.

This onslaught by Thomas Mann upon himself, this
sketch of his own fate, all the more damaging for its
mildly reasonable and even seductive tone, is replete with
aphorisms which have become famous. They struck
ruthlessly home to the hearts of those typical artists of
the period in Munich, among whom Mann so often, like
his hero among the dancers in the Danish hotel, had stood
silent. It is impossible for a healthy man to be an artist.
Does not every artist work better the worse he feels ?
Who can work in the Spring ? One must be positively
dead to life before one can work at all. Is an artist even
a man ? Is he not like the unsexed singers of the Vatican,
with nothing but their golden throats ? Is he not worse ?
A positive criminal, increasing the evil from which he
sprang ?

" I know a banker, a grey-haired business man, who
has a gift for writing stories. He employs this gift in
his idle hours and some of his stories are of the first rank.
But despite, I say, despite this excellent gift his withers are
by no means unwrung. On the contrary he has had to
serve a prison sentence on anything but trifling grounds.
Yes, it was actually first in prison that he became conscious of his gift and his experiences as a convict are the
main theme in all his works. One might be rash enough
to conclude that a man has to be at home in some kind of
gaol in order to become a poet. But can you escape the
suspicion that the source and essence of his being an

artist had less to do with his life in prison than they had with the reasons that brought him there ? A banker who writes, that is a rarity, isn't it ? But a banker who isn't a criminal, who is irreproachably respectable and yet writes, he doesn't exist." *

Lisaweta tells Kröger that these extravagant views of his are due to the fact that he is really no artist at all but a *bourgeois manqué*. He seems to accept this explanation, referring it later to his heredity, which is a pretty exact copy of Mann's own.

" My father, you know, had the temperament of the north, solid, reflective, puritanically correct, with a tendency to melancholia. My mother, of indeterminate foreign blood, was beautiful, sensuous, naive, passionate and careless at once, and, I think, irregular by instinct." †

It was Nietzsche who said that scepticism was the result of mixed breeding and Nietzsche who diagnosed decadence, the sickness of Europe, as scepticism. But this conclusion really begs the question which Thomas Mann has so much at heart. Every considerable artist who has ever lived has been " reflective . . . with a tendency to melancholia . . ." and also " naive, passionate and . . . irregular by instinct," as Mann found himself to be. But not every artist, not even Schiller, who set an antithesis between himself and Goethe not unlike Mann's, has concluded that he is therefore worthless and inhuman. In any case the mere existence of Heinrich

* Translation by H. T. Lowe-Porter. Martin Secker, 1928.
† Translation by H. T. Lowe-Porter.

Mann, who has no trace of his brother's dual nature, discounts the argument from heredity.

Tonio Kröger does not solve the problem of the relation of art to life. The terms of the syllogism are too simple. There never were such people as the all too simply Nietzschean Hans and Ingeborg, any more than there ever were such completely noble savages as Rousseau imagined. Nor has there ever been an artist such as Tonio Kröger—Mann himself is not one—whose spirit is merely criticism, negation, hostility to life.

Yet not even in *Buddenbrooks* was the issue made so clear. The rest of Mann's work was to deepen and complicate this central dichotomy, to multiply its mutual relationships and thus to bring it much nearer to a final resolution. But without the preliminary and forcible statement contained in *Tonio Kröger* the really orderly progress of the author's thought would have inevitably produced an effect of indecisive confusion.

Kröger was one of the tragic masks of art. Detlev Spinell in *Tristan*, the next most considerable of the stories in this collection, "a queer sort of man, with a name like some kind of mineral or precious stone," is one of its comic masks. Like Kröger he really is an artist. He has written a novel " of medium length with a perfectly bewildering drawing on the jacket, printed on a sort of filter paper . . . its scenes were laid in fashionable *salons*, in luxurious boudoirs, full of choice *objets d'art*, old furniture, Gobelins, rare porcelains, priceless stuffs and art treasures of all sorts and kinds. On the description of these things was expended the most loving care. As you read you constantly saw Herr Spinell with distended nostrils, saying, How beautiful ! My God, look, how beautiful !" * But Spinell is a figure of fun. He looks like a dissipated baby, has an indistinct and ridiculous way of speaking and walks upon enormous feet. He is staying at Dr. Leander's sanatorium. Mann's interest in such places, thus antedating his wife's sojourn at Davos by ten years, was later to have important consequences for his work. But Spinell is not sojourning under the Leander *régime* for any reason except that he finds the Empire style of the building and its furniture morally elevating. Gabriele Klöterjahn, the angelic wife of a coarsely epicurean business man, whom she adores, is also at the sanatorium. The surname, to a German ear, has an almost violently vulgar ring. Her case is believed to be a light one, a trifling affection of the trachea. Mann's medical knowledge, later to become extremely detailed, is already remarkable in a layman. Spinell revives the lady's interest in the piano, which she had foregone since her marriage. They find an arrangement of the " Liebestod " and she plays it, in the twilight.

The emotional strain of this experience, fostered by Spinell's attitude, turns the affection of the trachea to serious lung trouble. Herr Klöterjahn is summoned and arrives, with his and Gabriele's little boy, an exceedingly boisterous infant, not yet two years old. Spinell writes an extraordinary letter to the husband, though they are

* Translation by H. T. Lowe-Porter.

both under the same roof. Its composition was slow, " considering the man was a writer by trade, you would have drawn the conclusion, watching him, that a writer is one to whom writing comes harder than to anybody else." * The epistle is immensely long. Its gist is to inform Herr Klöterjahn that his wife is dying as a consequence of her marriage to him, to the " peasant gourmand."

" And if she does not go hence with your vulgarity upon her head ; if at the very last she has lifted herself out of the depths of degradation and passes into an ecstasy, with the deathly kiss of beauty on her brow— well, it is I, Sir, who have seen to that ! You, meanwhile, were probably spending your time with chambermaids in dark corners." *

The husband naturally visits the author of this singular communication and tells him with contemptuous fury what he thinks of him. This monologue—for Spinell hardly speaks a word—is interrupted by the dramatic announcement of Gabriele's death agony. The honest merchant rushes from the room. Spinell, to calm himself, goes for a walk and comes face to face with Klöterjahn junior in his perambulator. The magnificent baby greets the cadaverous novelist with excessive and terrifying mirth.

" Herr Spinell turned round and went thence. Pursued by the youthful Klöterjahn's joyous screams, he went away across the gravel, walking stiffly, yet not

* Translation by H. T. Lowe-Porter.

103

without grace : his gait was the hesitating gait of one who would disguise the fact that, inwardly, he is running away." *

Detlev Spinell is Hanno Buddenbrook as an adult. He is also much of Thomas Mann, whose double irony, as usual, does not spare himself. Arthur Holitscher, the Munich writer who was so aggrieved by this caricature, was not altogether right in his indignation. But no doubt certain details, for example the gait referred to in the paragraph just quoted, which ends the tale, were due to that famous, or infamous, opera-glass. Gabriele Klöterjahn has a touch of the " Bovaryism " of Toni Buddenbrook. The former, too, comes of a decadent burgher family. And, as in the novel, life triumphs, externally at any rate, over mind. Spinell is in the end defeated by Klöterjahn. The aesthete is a poor, cold creature, while the merchant is manly and warm-hearted.

In spite of Gabriele's death there is more comedy than tragedy in this story, though it is not so lightly written as the third in order of interest, *The Way to the Church-yard*. The style of this really painful narrative has such zest and grace that its full effect, like that of a nocturne by Chopin, is not realised until some time after the finished hearing. Piepsam—another of Mann's onomatopoeic names, which suits the feeble twittering of a sick bird—is an embittered and degenerate little man, not unlike Tobias Mindernickel. He is consumed by persecution mania, obsessed by the gross injustice of life and has taken

* Translation by H. T. Lowe-Porter.

seriously to drink, which had always been a vice with him, in his despair. He goes, one ironically bright Spring morning, to the churchyard in which the unseasonably deceased bodies of his wife and children lie. A blithe and gaily dressed young cyclist rides up behind him on the path, where cyclists have no business to be. Piepsam waves him back to the road. The cyclist rides on and knocks his mentor rudely on one side. The furious and miserable little wretch first tries to detain him, or to mount behind him, it is deliberately not quite clear which, then hurls a torrent of abuse after him, in which all his useless resentment at his fate finds expression, and at last falls unconscious in a paroxysm.

The cyclist is " life," cynical, indifferent, urgent as the wind, uncontrollable by words. Piepsam is the eternal outcast, the decadent, first cousin to the artist, though he neither paints nor writes and has no ear for music. The tale is only a sketch on the old theme. But its literary achievement is remarkable. No one but Thomas Mann could have presented with such infectious gaiety, yet with such profound sympathy that there is never the least lapse from good taste, an episode which returns to the reader's mind in the guise of a lamentable and even squalid horror.

Gladius Dei is another mixture of comedy and tragedy. Hieronymus, the monk of Munich, the " Sword of God," a first study for that Girolamo Savonarola who was to be a later hero of Thomas Mann, is discovered in the sunny market place which Mann knew so well, at odds with the art which he sees about him and more particularly in the picture-shop window of Herr Blüthenzweig, where there is a Madonna that outrages his religious sentiments. The model, he overhears the crowd say, was a well known " little milliner," the mistress of the artist. The figure of the Virgin is to his mind improperly aphrodisiac. Three days later he bursts into the shop to make his protest. " Art," he cries, " is the divine fire sent to kindle the earth, that it may burst into flame and be destroyed with all its disgrace and agony, in redeeming pity." The sentence was to be used again by Mann in the great drama to which *Gladius Dei* is a prelude. But it makes no impression on the shopkeeper. Hieronymus is ignominiously ejected and stands muttering, in his visions, on the hard pavement thronged by the gay crowds of the German Athens.

The monk and his peculiar morality are not taken quite seriously, though he is not altogether an unsympathetic figure. There is much to be said, as Mann himself had felt in his early Munich days, against the artist who is a craftsman and nothing more and who uses his skill to subvert decent and legitimate feeling. But the interesting point of the narrative lies in the dexterous and hitherto not anticipated manipulation of the antithesis. Here Hieronymus himself stands for mind, the reflective, sensitive, serious temper of the true aesthete, and the bohemians who reject him for Nietzschean " life," the crude, irresponsible, mocking spirit of one kind of *bourgeois*. The contrast is now less that of the artist with the Philistine than that of the seer, the prophet, with the man of the world. Much was to come of this new direction given to an old problem.

In *The Wardrobe* the reader finds himself in yet another sphere. It is the sphere of Hans Andersen, of the Hoffmann of the *Tales*, of the post-romantic poet—in a different sense from that of the neo-romanticism cultivated by Mann—Hugo von Hofmannsthal. *The Wardrobe* is a dream, a fairy story, strange to the limit of the grotesque. In spirit it resembles *Death*, the weakest of the earlier narratives. Albrecht van der Qualen—the name is again significant, *Qualen* being the German for torment or distress—is condemned by the doctors. He loses all sense of time and space, throws his watch away and wanders through Germany. He alights at a wayside station and hires a room for the night. The room resembles that which Mann occupied in his early youth at Munich. Albrecht van der Qualen finds in the wardrobe a phantom, the apparition of a beautiful naked woman, who for several nights, like Scheherazade, tells him a melancholy tale and then vanishes. He desires to touch her, but finds that when he does, though she does not repulse him, the next night the wardrobe is empty.

This piece is a slight but moving elegy on the eternal elusiveness of the objects of man's desire. His desperate, abstracted yearning lives on in forever unfulfilled dreams that take what seems a concrete form. Tonio Kröger had said that a man must die to life in order to be a creator. But Albrecht van der Qualen longs for contact with the strange life that appears to him in the guise of the phantom woman. It is true that he can take her in his arms for a moment. But in the end she eludes him and he is again face to face with death.

The weird, sad, typically old-German atmosphere sustained throughout this little study is a note that Mann hardly ever touches again to this extent, though it intrudes at intervals in his work. There is a certain sentimentality, though a charming variety of such feeling, about the story, to English ears. Yet, as always, the literary art is unexceptionable and bathos is entirely absent.

In *Luischen* Mann returns to the familiar society of the cynical and the sensitive. Lawyer Jacoby is a colossus physically, but something of a cry-baby. His wife is what is or used to be known in Hollywoodian circles as a " vamp." She is beautiful and heartless. She takes a comic revenge, which ends in tragedy, upon her clumsy husband, when he implores her to behave more decently to him. At a wild party she persuades him to dress up as a little girl and then sing and dance to her and her pianist-lover. In the course of this ridiculous performance the respectable lawyer perceives the truth of the situation. The lover gives a cynically touching style to the piano accompaniment of the song and the husband's ear is sensitive enough to detect it. He had hitherto refused to believe in the reality of his wife's scorn and indifference towards him. The cruel enlightenment breaks his heart and he collapses in the middle of the song and dance and dies.

The story is the weakest of the six and has no point that Mann had not already made. Yet it is both amusing and tragically moving, according to the typical Mann recipe, of which he alone has the secret. The reader scarcely knows whether to laugh or to cry, and the more he ponders his text the further off he is from a conclusion. If art were no more than the photography of life *Luischen* would be a perfect example of it. As it is, the tale is indecisive and has little more than a merely repetitive significance in Mann's work. He had done all this before.

The idea of decadence, first dealt with in the volume entitled *Little Herr Friedemann*, transferred to a larger canvas in *Buddenbrooks* and still more curiously analysed in the *Tristan* collection, was now a fully elaborated instrument in the thought of Thomas Mann. Through it he could hold life in the balance and test its innumerable responses. Nietzsche, Schopenhauer and Wagner had done their work in him and led him to the threshold of a great creative career in which a synthesis, a solution would have to be sought of a problem that by 1905, the year of Mann's marriage, and his own thirtieth, had been so exhaustively stated. The burgher and the aesthete, north and south, man and woman, body and mind, life and art, stood face to face. So far the battle had scarcely begun. Some skirmishes had led to disasters fit to be lamented by poets. There had been a long engagement in which the issue still remained doubtful, though the literary embodiment of this conflict bore a significantly lugubrious sub-title. Its consequent repercussions, too,

seemed in general to confirm the results of the brief preliminary actions. But there was much, it was very evident, that had still to be said.

At all events the chronicler of this spiritual war was
himself an artist. So much was obvious, though it was
not quite so clear what sort of an artist he really was.
Tolstoy and Turgenev, Flaubert and the Goncourts, had
gone to the making of that style, already mature in *Little
Herr Friedemann*, which was a compound of realism and
romanticism, life and sympathy with death, humour and
the gravity of an aristocrat in a classic age.

With a mind already so richly found in contrasting
elements, with a weapon already so many-sided and
finely tempered, a man of thirty, who has just made a
singularly happy marriage, might do a great deal.
Thomas Mann, during the next five years alone, did more
than his most favourable critics expected and did it in
ways that neither they nor anybody else could have, with
the slightest degree of confidence, foretold.

CHAPTER II
THE PROBLEM OF HAPPINESS

MANN had shown in the first part of *Buddenbrooks* that he was plentifully endowed with the historical imagination. The period 1835-1855 was already history to the readers of 1901. The boy writer had dreamed of sixty-year-old Lübeck in contemporary Rome. And five years after he had left Rome his Italian experience began to haunt his fancy. The enthusiasm of his brother for the High Renaissance, the figure of that brother himself, grew more and more vivid and significant to him. The first fruit of these meditations was *Gladius Dei*. The harvest was *Fiorenza*, the three-act prose drama, dealing with the relations between Savonarola and Lorenzo the Magnificent, which was published in 1906.

When the play opens the priest, with his eloquent denunciations of the frivolity of the art-loving Florentines, is already making trouble in the city. There are riots; statues and paintings are destroyed by Fra Girolamo's fanatical followers; the preacher even dares to abuse publicly, in the cathedral, the fair and frail Fiore Strozzi, at that moment the mistress of Lorenzo himself. The despot, who is already on his death-bed, summons Savonarola to shrive him. The conversation which follows is the pith of the play. It was the most brilliant and profound which Mann had yet written. At last Lorenzo breaks down. The prior strides out, leaving him to his death.

The scene of the first Act is the study of Giovanni de' Medici, the seventeen-year-old Cardinal-aesthete, in the Villa Medici near Florence. Poliziano, his tutor, the celebrated humanist, who once saved the life of Giovanni's father, the great Lorenzo, is annoyed with his young pupil for finding the prior of San Marco, Girolamo Savonarola, more interesting than Plato. The preacher amuses the delicate young aristocrat, but infuriates the pedagogue. Pico della Mirandola, a noble humanist more favourably disposed to the fiery priest, enters to tell the story of the scandal in the Cathedral. In an eloquent narrative he describes Savonarola's Biblical invective against the fair city, the Scarlet Woman, the great Whore of Babylon, and how the prior turned upon Fiore, when she made a late and disturbing, but splendid, entry into the church, and transferred his epithets to her. Poliziano points out the political significance of the scene. Fra Girolamo, he is convinced, is bent upon the ruin of the Medici. But Pico, who had advised Lorenzo to summon the famous friar to Florence, laughs at him. Why should not morality again become fashionable, he asks, now that we have vulgarised beauty?

The second Act is laid in the magnificent gardens of the Villa. There is a lively scene, very amusing, between the genial, child-like artists who form an important part of Lorenzo's court and the despot's mistress, that brilliant and subtle beauty. Fiore ends by telling them that Savonarola is to visit Lorenzo that evening. The three protagonists of the first scene enter, after the lady's departure, and the political and social unrest of the city is again discussed. The humanists are sent for by the tyrant. Piero de' Medici, Giovanni's military elder brother, appears, and arrogantly dismisses the artists. He then vainly tries to borrow money from Giovanni and boasts of his coming glory. Giovanni escapes and Fiore again enters. There is a scene of high comedy between the beautiful and clever courtesan and the blunderingly amorous son of her patron. She laughs at him, telling him he is no hero, as he thinks. The true hero, she says, is the weak man whose fiery spirit nevertheless enables him to win the laurel. And she adds that two heroes of this type are going to fight for her that very evening.

In the third Act the despot is seated in his bedchamber, surrounded by his friends. A citizen of Florence enters with tidings of the troubles fostered by Savonarola. Lorenzo refuses to take the news seriously and tells his friends, after the worthy man's departure, how he had vainly tried to add the prior to their number. The next ominous visitor is a young apprentice of Botticelli. He informs the horrified audience of his master's conversion by the friar, destruction of his last picture and determination to devote himself to religious subjects in future. The tyrant dismisses his friends and sends for his sons. He begs Piero to preserve the beauty which has been created by the Medici in Florence, the beauty which the despot has always believed to stand above law and virtue. After the departure of the boys the dying man soliloquises in a passage of melancholy splendour, exalting the eternal strength of desire and depreciating the unnerving illusion of possession. Again Fiore, that incarnation of the gay, sophisticated city, enters. She tells the story of Savonarola's early passion for her, how she rejected the sallow and sickly little student he then was and drove him into the cloister. She adds that she has already summoned the priest to Lorenzo's presence, where he will be in the power of the ruler of Florence. The artists return, and in the midst of a Boccaccian tale by one of them the stern prior is announced. Lorenzo and his dark antagonist are left alone. The great dialogue begins. The tyrant asks for a definition of evil. Everything, the priest tells him, in us and outside us, which contradicts the spirit. And what do you mean by spirit? asks Lorenzo. The strength, replies Savonarola, which is bent upon the achievement of purity and peace. The prince exclaims that he and the prior are brothers, that Savonarola, too, is an artist. No, a prophet, returns the other, an artist who has become a saint. For art, he adds in the words of Hieronymus in *Gladius Dei*, is " the fire of destruction and redemption. Beauty and spirit are enemies. Spirit may long for beauty. The hours of weakness, of self-betrayal and of sweet shame are such hours of longing. For beauty is glad and delectable and strong. It is life. It will never understand spirit, will be rejected by it, will even perhaps fear it, repulse it with aversion, scoff at it without mercy and so in the end drive it back upon itself." *

" I hear the melody of my life," says Lorenzo sadly. He is sinking fast. The confession of sins commences. The prince entrusts his beloved city to the care of the priest. But Savonarola's evident triumph brings reaction. Suddenly Lorenzo cries, " The spirit you talk of is death ! Art is the life of all life ! " He falls back, calling for help, for arms to slay the traitor. The greedy, ambitious prior must die. But with the crowd that pours into the room come messengers to report that the citizens are marching on the Villa to rescue Savonarola, of whose danger they have heard rumours. Fiore warns the priest against ambition and threatens him with the stake. But the preacher stalks out to his fate with the words, " I love fire," upon his lips.

Fiorenza is the first resolute attempt by Mann to solve the great problem, which he had so often stated, of the relation of art to life. *Gladius Dei* had already given the question a new turn and it is now seen to carry the terms of a synthesis whose establishment will show mankind how to be happy. It cannot be said that the matter is here satisfactorily settled. The protagonists, the seer and the man of the world, are in reality far too much alike. Both are physically weak and ugly. Lorenzo, the sensualist, cannot even appreciate perfumes properly, and he is dying. The preacher, when he is out of the pulpit, is

* Author's translation.

so exhausted that he can do nothing but lie on his bed. Fiore Strozzi calls him, in his unofficial hours, Mr. Deadman. Both the prophet and the prince, again, are spiritual brothers in the self-torture that arises in them from their sense of the eternal dualism of this world and the kingdom of heaven.

Savonarola, in fact, who is really the principal personage in the drama, is such a mass of contradictions that his character makes unreal and chaotic the synthesis which seems to be the main purpose of the action. If he is the first definite imperative in Thomas Mann's work he is an unconvincing one. In the first two Acts he appears as a single-souled saint and hero, an ascetic, pure intellect, an artist only in so far as he is consumed by a fire of zeal for the truth. In the third Act Fiore reveals that in his youth he had made love to her and been rejected, and that this is the cause of his devotion to the cloister, while Lorenzo himself had enabled him to reach the Cathedral pulpit. Common passions and worldly ambition begin to show through the fanatic mask. The priest himself admits that fame is sweet and the mob contemptible. It is clear that he is already at heart the dictator of Florence which he was to become in reality after Lorenzo's death. His pride and force of will are Nietzschean, there is actually nothing about him of the Nazarene whom Heine would have been ready to see in his contrast with the Hellenic Lorenzo.

Yet this character, which finally appears, to speak frankly, as that of an intolerable hypocrite, is treated with

almost exactly reproduced in his stories. And a certain malice is not always entirely excluded. But in any case the point is quite a minor one. Mann does not, like a great many modern novelists, speak only to his acquaintances in the first half of the twentieth century, but to the world and to posterity.

In the interval which elapsed between *Fiorenza* and the appearance of a further major work by Thomas Mann a volume entitled *Little Herr Friedemann and Other Tales* was published. It reprinted the title story, also *The Will to Happiness*, *Disappointment*, *Der Bajazzo*, *Tobias Mindernickel*, and *Luischen*, with two new narratives, *The Famished* and *The Railway Accident*.

The Famished relates how a bored *noceur* leaves one of those resorts which cater for all the sensual appetites of city dwellers. He is in love with a girl who is dancing in the building, a member of that cheerful, shallow and irresistibly seductive sister-and-brotherhood, representatives of which are so often met with in Mann's pages. If only just for to-night, he meditates, I were not an artist, but a human being, a Man ! If only I could get rid of that inexorable curse laid upon the maker of beauty : thou shalt not be, thou shalt observe, thou shalt not live, thou shalt create, thou shalt not love, thou shalt understand. What is intelligence, after all ? Only hate playing a game with life. What is art ? Only desire building castles in the air.

So he dreams, at two o'clock on a winter's morning, as he lights a cigarette and calls a cab. Then he catches sight of a strange-looking proletarian lounging against a lamp-post and staring at him. He sees envy in the man's expression. What an utter misunderstanding! If he only knew! Nothing more happens. The author, for that is the *noceur's* profession, is driven home and the story, if it can be called one, ends.

The episode is trifling in itself, but in its presentation the reader is conscious of a new development in the thought of Thomas Mann. He had affirmed often enough that an artist is an outcast from society. But to identify him spiritually with a beggar was another matter. The young writer in this tale is led to reflect upon the resemblance between himself and the wretched creature he meets. Both are hungry, the proletarian for the dull physical objects the gentleman has just left in disgust, the latter for an ideal which, he meditates, is perhaps equally illusory. Is not his own irritant longing for Lilli and what she stands for as misdirected as the tramp's? Are not all the desires of men as vain as his own? In any case all men are brothers in their common misery, though their misery may be due to infinitely different causes. An artist should not be an aristocrat, a Buddenbrook, a Lorenzo, he should be a plebeian, whose business is not to live in the sense of enjoying the good things of life, but to hate, to mock and to desire.

Detlef in *The Famished* is a serious person, a real elegiac hero, perhaps a preliminary sketch, in spite of the later date of publication, for Tonio Kröger, the Thomas Mann of the period 1900-1905. At all events he stands, as Kröger did, between the two distinct worlds of life and art and finds that life is, on the whole, the preferable world. The idea of the beggar-artist was not to be explicitly elaborated in Mann's later work. It did not, however, disappear, but became absorbed in a larger view, which was already about to be promulgated.

The Railway Accident is not an important story. Like *Disappointment* and *Der Bajazzo* it is a tale of the confessional variety, but a comedy. It illustrates comparatively simply and directly the old antithesis of the familiar and the strange, and attempts no intellectual judgments. One of Mann's rare pieces of pure satire appears in the portrait of the perfect gentleman in the train, who is so haughty with the guard and so upset by the accident. No one is hurt, but the narrator has a valuable manuscript in the luggage van and it is said, at first, that the van has been destroyed. This report turns out in the end to be untrue, but meanwhile the agitated proprietor and perpetrator of the script has resolved that he will write it all over again, if need be, and perhaps even better than before. He is contrasted with the amusingly conceited and selfish dandy who took the accident as a purely personal affair.

The most striking event in the literary life of Thomas Mann since *Buddenbrooks* was now pending. A novel entitled *Royal Highness* appeared in 1909. The most contradictory valuations of this performance were at once disseminated and are still current. Some declared that the great synthesis had at last been discovered, that the act of creation was complete and that there was no more to be said. Others were puzzled by a fantastic farrago that did not seem to mean anything, unless it were designed to exhibit the author's sense of humour. A third section were openly contemptuous of a sentimental fairy tale, a Ruritanian romance. Mann himself, some twenty years later, appeared to disparage in the book a certain artificiality.

It is not probable that Thomas Mann had ever read the English novel published by Anthony Hope in 1894, *The Prisoner of Zenda*. If he had, the fact would not detract from any literary value that *Royal Highness* may possess. For he could not have taken much more from *The Prisoner* than the idea of an imaginary small independent State in the heart of Europe.

The twentieth century German Grand Duchy he here creates is in a backward condition through financial troubles, though the inhabitants are honest and industrious. The prince who eventually accedes is a decent young fellow, not overburdened with brains, though having a certain amount of intelligent curiosity. His quietly watchful and enquiring eye, coupled with a certain bluntness of exterior, makes him look rather like a chauffeur. At any rate he is much more like any of his subjects than he is like any other member of the reigning house. His tutor, the hideous but genial Dr. Überbein, takes advantage of this fact to attempt a realisation of his theory that a prince must not be anything but an exact representative of his people. Klaus Heinrich is brought up to embody this dry and narrow ideal. But a German-American millionaire, Spoelmann, with his beautiful, clever and headstrong daughter Imma, break in upon this situation. The lady takes the prince in hand, the financial magnate attends to the internal economy of the country. The suicide of the mortified Überbein does not much disturb the musical comedy ending, complete with wedding bells and a cheering populace.

In a preface the reader is introduced to Prince Klaus Heinrich, who " has narrow shoulders, dark hair and the wide cheek-bones so common in this part of the world, blue, rather tired-looking eyes, and a boyish face with a kind but reserved expression." * But the first chapter begins with the circumstances of his birth. His mother is the beautiful Grand Duchess Dorothea, his father the Grand Duke Johann Albrecht III. The ideal Klaus Heinrich is to fulfil is enunciated : " The people want to see their best, their highest, their dream, what stands for their soul, represented in their princes." * The boy is born with a crippled left hand, due to stunted growth in the womb. But there is a gipsy prophecy that a prince with one hand will do the realm more good than all the rest could with two. The decadent charm of the Grand Duchy, bankrupt below the delightful surface, is symbolised by a rose-tree that grows in the courtyard of an old castle. Its flowers are exceptionally beautiful, but have no scent, only a strange odour of decay. Klaus Heinrich grows up in an atmosphere of old-fashioned

* Translation by A. Cecil Curtis. Sidgwick and Jackson, 1916.

court etiquette, knowing nothing of the outer world. He and his younger sister Ditlinde become inseparable and play together, as Thomas and Heinrich Mann played, in deserted rooms full of memories of a bygone age. The elder brother, Albrecht, the Heir Apparent, is sickly and reserved. In the course of time Klaus Heinrich achieves a private tutor, Raoul Überbein, who "had a red beard and a greenish-white complexion, with watery blue eyes, thin red hair and unusually ugly, protruding, sharp-pointed ears." * This strange person enunciates explicitly for his pupil the philosophy of representation which must govern his career as a prince. " Representing," says he, " is naturally something more and higher than merely being. One has to stand for a number, be the exalted and refined expression of a multitude." *

The Grand Duke dies of a strange, almost abstract malady, a sort of decomposition of the blood. Albrecht succeeds, but his ill-health and his cynical temperament soon lead him to delegate his duties to Klaus Heinrich, who is much more popular than his brother. The ageing Grand Duchess Dorothea struggles in vain to preserve her marvellous beauty and at last goes into eccentric retirement. Ditlinde marries a prince who has exchanged princedom for a commercial career. But Klaus Heinrich remains a ruler, a representative.

" His way of sitting in his carriage was quite peculiar. He did not lean back indolently and comfortably on the cushions, but took just as active a part in the motions of

* Translation by A. Cecil Curtis.

the carriage, when driving, as in those of his horse when riding. With his hands crossed on his sword-hilt and one foot advanced he, as it were, took the unevennesses of the ground and accommodated himself to the motion of the badly hung carriage." *

This attitude is contrasted with that of Albrecht II, his almost invisible brother, who finds the idea of representation ridiculous and compares himself, in his princely aspect, with a well-known local " character," whose harmless mania it is to supervise the starting of trains at railway stations, though his antics are in reality completely ignored by the actual authorities.

About this time Klaus Heinrich has an interview with Axel Martini, the poet who has won prizes for his magnificent compositions in praise of life. Martini " had rather staring eyes, thin cheeks and a dark yellow moustache, which was clipped like a hedge. His hair was already quite grey on the temples, although . . . he was not more than thirty years old. Under his eyes glowed patches of red, which did not suggest robust health." * He tells Klaus Heinrich that " Unsuitability for everything else is the sole proof of the poetic calling. Poetry is the expression and refuge of that unsuitability." * He adds that " I am convinced that my talent is inseparably connected with my bodily infirmity." * The prince comes to the conclusion that this gentleman is " certainly a little repulsive." *

The momentous event which is to make history in the Duchy now occurs. Samuel N. Spoelmann buys one of

* Translation by A. Cecil Curtis.

the Grand Ducal castles and establishes himself as a
resident in the bankrupt country. He is, like most
millionaires, a shabby little man with nothing particularly
striking about him. Most people take the great man to
be Spoelmann's private physician, a genial, lantern-jawed
American, Dr. Watercloose. The name of the most
famous of all British inventions is irresistibly comic to
the continental ear. Mann himself had already used it for
a minor character in *Buddenbrooks*. Spoelmann possesses,
besides Dr. Watercloose and a very noisy but aristocratic
Scotch collie, a daughter of nineteen with a pearly complexion, large black eyes, a resolute temperament and
considerable mathematical aptitude. She it is who is to
change the history of Ruritania. Dr. Überbein does not
seem to like her, but he tells Klaus Heinrich, who has
already seen her, with more than approval, several times,
that she is visiting the hospital he is to inspect. The two
young people, representatives of the old and the new
world, meet. The stiff courtesy of the prince is countered
by the dry humour of the young American. Klaus Heinrich visits the Spoelmanns and his infatuation grows
steadily, though the millionaire is brusque and morose,
not to say boorish, and Imma distinctly contradictory in
her conversation. The mathematics, too, are rather a
formidable obstacle to love-making. The description of
a page of Imma's algebra notebook is a good example
of Mann's extraordinary capacity for making dry detail
vivid and amusing.

" There were Greek and Latin letters of various heights,

crossed and cancelled, arranged above and below crossed lines, covered by other lines, enclosed in round brackets, formulated in square brackets. Single letters, pushed forward like sentries, kept guard above the main bodies. Cabalistic signs, quite unintelligible to the lay mind, cast their arms round letters and ciphers while fractions stood in front of them and ciphers and letters hovered round their tops and bottoms. Strange syllables, abbreviations of mysterious words, were scattered everywhere. Between the columns were written sentences and remarks in ordinary language, whose sense was equally beyond the normal intelligence and conveyed no more to the reader than an incantation." *

In spite of the algebra Klaus Heinrich's love assumes such proportions that he falls completely under Imma's influence and his artificiality warms to a genuine humanity. At last there is a declaration, the young people study economics together and the strange wooing finally issues in a betrothal. On the day of the announcement of the news Überbein commits suicide.

It is not difficult to see Fräulein Katja Pringsheim, Thomas Mann's bride of 1905, in the fairy princess Imma, with her brisk wit, brunette beauty and mathematical talent. Nor the bachelor Thomas Mann himself in the pedantic Überbein, who comes to a bad end when his hitherto docile pupil becomes a Man and an individual under Imma's less official instruction. There are other familiar figures. For example, the prize court poet

* Translation by A. Cecil Curtis.

Martini, who writes splendid hymns in praise of joy but does not dare to drink the wine in the cup which is his reward. He is the brother of Tonio Kröger, Detlev Spinell and the hero of *The Famished*. But, on the whole, this book relies far less on immediate personal experience than anything Mann had yet written. It is a fairy tale in the sense that there is very little satire in it, though of course plenty of irony, and that almost no character is very much less than agreeable, even Martini and the unfortunate Dr. Überbein. Yet the characteristic Mannian irony entirely anticipates the slightest thought of the nursery. The personages live a real life and resemble real people. If a smile scarcely ever leaves the lips of the reader of *Royal Highness* it is the smile with which he regards the human comedy, not the tender grimace of half melancholy condescension with which the adult approaches juvenile literature.

This flight from the bonds of everyday personal experience was an achievement for the apologist of *Bilse and I*, though he could already point to *Fiorenza*, the tragedy, as the present novel was the comedy, of high imagination. Comedy it was, as Mann himself has called it. But there was much reflection in it ; enthusiasts said it contained profounder and more practical thought than any of the previous work. Political economy, ethics, education and the nature of love are exhaustively and entertainingly discussed. It really does look as though Imma Spoelmann were the long-sought synthesis between art and life. This is the view of the small but select body of criticism which regards the rest of Mann's work as a declension from the height of this " perfect and lovely " tale. The ultimate verdict will depend upon the judge's personal inclination to optimism or pessimism. In any event the case for optimism is here stated as finely and convincingly as only a thinker familiar with the dark depths of Schopenhauer could utter it.

Klaus Heinrich, lonely as none but princes and poets, those necessarily " representative men," can be, is saved from the atrophy of his fate by love. Love has bridged the Nietzschean gulf between art and life. Can anyone be ignorant of life, the honest youth asks, rhetorically, who is acquainted with Love ? Unlike the Buddenbrooks the Grand Ducal family will be preserved from decadence by this magic power. No longer need the prince, like the ill-starred Thomas Buddenbrook, act a lie, in his desperate pride, to conceal the canker at his heart. He may with a good conscience find pleasure in a real sacrifice of himself, perpetually renewed, to his people, in the name of love. This was a confession of democratic faith which pleased Heinrich Mann. The idea of service to humanity, so prominent in Goethe and Schiller, is here for the first time explicit in Thomas Mann and was not again to leave him, though it was not in future to assume such isolated force as in *Royal Highness*. Goethe, in fact, with his *Elective Affinities*, with his " duty can do much, love infinitely more," presides over this book as Schopenhauer, Nietzsche and Wagner had presided over earlier works. It is true that the great man would have laughed at Martini and looked round for a poet who dared to live. But the laughter of Thomas Mann mingles with Goethe's, though he does not provide his senior's requirement, perhaps because, for the moment, that requirement was Thomas Mann himself.

The subordinate ideas in this bright and clear affirmation of life in all its extensions support the main theme. There is the old preoccupation with the grotesque. But here it can be seen to be lovable. Klaus Heinrich's left hand is withered, Spoelmann, whose wealth makes him and his daughter almost as lonely as princes or poets, looks like a scarecrow, plays the organ and collects glass. Überbein tells his charge that it is more important to him to be able to hold a teacup properly than to be a mathematician. The education of the prince, to be rather than to do, to put the person above the thing, resulting in the production of form empty of content, is contrasted with the education of the burgher, to do rather than to be, to put the thing above the person, resulting in the production of content unorganised by form. Imma, the bourgeois princess, unites in herself the two systems and will be henceforth, through love, the exemplar for Klaus Heinrich.

This modern Cyropaedia and " All for Love," presenting like Garrick or Sir Barry Jackson in their treatment of Shakespeare an eternal theme in contemporary dress, is in style a perfect instance of Mann's fresh, vivid and exact writing. If it is artificial, as the author afterwards, perhaps half jestingly, declared, it is also art.

Whatever may be thought by pessimistic philosophers of the content of *Royal Highness* the book is, in form at any rate, a masterpiece.

Although the fragment, *Confessions of the Arch Swindler Felix Krull*, was not actually made public until 1922 it really belongs in spirit to this period of Thomas Mann's life. He was engaged upon it at intervals between the years 1909 and 1914. As the title indicates it purports to be yet another of those autobiographical disclosures in the form of which Mann, like Musset, Stendhal and Dostoievsky, discerned a high literary value. The composition was interrupted by other more important work and by the war. It deals, in its present state, only with the childhood of the central figure, who can hardly, yet, be called a hero. But the zest and solidity of the piece arouse a hope in the reader that even at this late hour a sequel may be forthcoming. The actor motive, which is always prominent in Mann's work and had been used with notable effect in *Buddenbrooks* and *Royal Highness*, is here further developed. We all know the type of actor who is a god on the stage and a demon or an idiot off it. Which is the real man ? Krull was fascinated by the fact that such dualism was possible. He saw that acting—the Greeks called it by a name from which our " hypocrisy " is derived—fulfils a need of humanity, as profound as it is remarkable, for self-deception. *Vulgus vult decipi.* So many people seem to long so ardently to be illuded, and are so pleased when their yearnings are satisfied that one may be forgiven for supposing that illusion may be a law of nature. If so, it is clear that happiness, beauty, even the sort of truth to which mankind may attain, is not possible without some kind of trickery. The very falseness of outlook which Mann had been so concerned to expose to the scorn of his public in *Buddenbrooks*, in those misguided burgher and burgher-artist temperaments, he here seems to accept as indispensable.

Felix Krull, in a literary sense, is the *coup de grâce* inflicted by Thomas Mann on the naturalism of the Zolaists, with which he had never been quite comfortable. Romance of some kind, some sort of illusion, for the contentment of mankind, must be brought back to life and to artistic expression. In sociology, as Goethe had seen, crime is the most obvious example of it. The unprecedented fury of enthusiasm with which a de-romanticised Europe has seized upon the " detective " novel, is significant in this connection.

The idea of the close relation of artist and criminal, already noted by Tonio Kröger, here receives a further consolidation. Plato himself had considered poets little better than swindlers, the most convincing of Shakespeare's villains are far from prosaic. And every Freudian knows that scribbling and versifying criminals are the rule and not the exception.

So far it is permissible to interpret the adolescent reflections of Felix Krull. It is all rather mystifyingly playful and ironic, a charming parody on the traditional German education-novel, which began a crowded career with *Wilhelm Meister*. What the great moralist-author is ultimately to make of this lusty literary suckling remains a problem unless and until the final chapter of the *Confessions* is written.

The problem of happiness grew out of the idea of decadence in the mind of Thomas Mann. Mankind, Europe at all events, was sick, as Nietzsche had proclaimed. Could it be cured? If so, how, and to what sort of health might it be expected to return?

Fiorenza had delved deep into this question. *Royal Highness* had appeared to solve it by means of the reagent of love. It remained to be seen whether the solution was permanent, or whether it required a further analysis, which might lead to a fresh and profounder statement of a perhaps eternal antithesis.

CHAPTER III
THE ADVENTURE OF BEAUTY

THE four chief works of Thomas Mann up to the end of the first decade of the present century had each in their turn been very generally acclaimed. But there were still some few dissentients. *Buddenbrooks* reproduced too many actual incidents and people : *Tonio Kröger* was overburdened with a too narrow melancholy : *Fiorenza* ranted : there was artifice and comic opera in *Royal Highness* : such complaints were not altogether without foundation, though they could be, and were, pressed too far. But on the publication of *Death in Venice*, a tale of well under thirty thousand words—*Tonio Kröger* has something over twenty thousand—the most hostile critic could not for a long time find his voice.

To turn from *Royal Highness* to *Death in Venice* is like passing from Fragonard to Rembrandt. The ripple of summer lightning changes to the sombre gradients of a winter sunset. The successive tones, rich and distant as those of some five-hundred-year-old portrait in oils, draw the reader on by carefully blended stages to the inevitable catastrophe, which, when it comes, falls quietly into its place in the whole picture, sealing and stamping the general impression like the last chorus in a Greek tragedy.

That impression is manifold. A new, sustained seriousness, a temporary farewell to the celebrated Mannian irony, a new technique that almost abandons the *leitmotiv*, a turning away from objective experience to the abstraction of a personality. Gustav von Aschenbach, the hero, is a mature Tonio Kröger. He is a man of fifty, a far-famed writer, a classic of German prose, who has outgrown the cynical despair, the effete decadence and moral nihilism of his youth, and by rejecting, like Savonarola, the illusions of earthly knowledge and passion, to trust only his intuition, has reached rebirth upon a lonely height of inspiration. But he has paid the price of supreme artistic achievement. He is physically worn out by the struggle for perfection. Yet, true to the traditions of his Prussian ancestors, soldiers and servants of the State, he still holds his head erect and incarnates the significance of his favourite word, " Endure," the motto also of Frederick the Great, on whose life Aschenbach had written one of his most famous novels. Nietzsche would have approved this modern, dispassionate pilgrim of the decadence and used him as a stick with which to beat the unregenerate Wagner, in his final quarrel with that fiery musician.

During the course of an afternoon walk in Munich, where Aschenbach lives, he perceives an outlandish-looking figure standing in the portico of the mortuary chapel of the North Cemetery. The man, who has the appearance of a tourist, seems to stare at him in rather a sinister way, showing his teeth. Aschenbach finds, as he proceeds homeward, that he has an irresistible desire to travel to the East. After an abortive expedition to an island in the Adriatic, which does not please him, he embarks, in a rainy dawn, for Venice. One of the passengers on the far from luxurious steamer is an unpleasant character, an old man who has got himself up to look like a youth, and attempts to behave like one. This rowdy and equivocal personage sheds, in Aschenbach's weary brain, a curious but appropriate air of abnormality upon his journey to the ambiguous landscape, lovely and decayed, half Asiatic, half Dutch in its natural constituents, half Moorish, half Gothic in its architecture. The distinguished novelist, on his arrival, hires a gondola to take him to the steamer which is to convey him to the Lido. The gondolier, however, a rather odd-looking person, evidently not of Italian stock, wilfully misunderstands the order and takes Aschenbach direct across the lagoon to his destination. The preoccupied passenger is too tired to resist. At the landing he finds he has no small change and goes to get some at the hotel. When he returns to pay the gondolier the latter has vanished. An old boatman tells Aschenbach that the man was known to have no licence and was probably afraid of being arrested.

In the lounge of the Lido hotel where the novelist stays he observes a Polish family, mother, governess, three nondescript girl-children and a boy about fourteen, the latter of striking beauty.

" His face recalled the noblest moment of Greek sculpture—pale, with a sweet reserve, with clustering, honey-coloured ringlets, the brow and nose descending in one line, the winning mouth, the expression of pure and god-like serenity. Yet, with all this chaste perfection of form, it was of such unique personal charm that the observer thought he had never seen, either in nature or art, anything so utterly happy and consummate." *

The aesthete is strongly moved, in the spirit of a connoisseur, by this vision, and continues to observe it during the next day or two, noting that the lad's health seems to be as delicate as the distinction of his appearance. But Aschenbach's own physique is giving him trouble, the air does not suit him and he decides to leave. However, his luggage, at the last moment, is despatched in the wrong direction. He has already regretted his decision, for the wind has changed and he feels better. The *contretemps* leads him to make up his mind to stay after all, enjoy the improved weather, and contemplate Tadzio. He has gathered that such is the name of the Polish charmer.

As he watches the boy playing on the beach he thinks of the Platonic dialogue entitled *Phaedrus*, of the scene beneath the ancient plane-tree outside the walls of Athens, of the smooth stream Achelous, of the grassy slope upon which Socrates discoursed to his young friend on the nature of virtue and desire.

" For beauty, my Phaedrus, beauty alone is lovely and

* Translation by H. T. Lowe-Porter. Martin Secker, 1928.

visible at once. For, mark you, it is the sole aspect of the spiritual which we can perceive through our senses, or bear so to perceive. Else, what should become of us, if the divine, if reason and virtue and truth, were to speak to us through the senses ? Should we not perish and be consumed by love, as Semele aforetime was by Zeus ? So beauty, then, is the beauty-lover's way to the spirit— but only the way, only the means, my little Phaedrus. . . ."

" And then, sly arch-lover that he was, he said the subtlest thing of all : that the lover was nearer the divine than the beloved ; for the god was in the one but not in the other—perhaps the tenderest, most mocking thought that ever was thought, and source of all the guile and secret bliss the lover knows." *

When, at last, Tadzio gives his middle-aged admirer an innocent and ravishing smile, such a smile as that of Narcissus, a smile that men cannot endure and that the gods do not allow to mortals, the grey-haired, respectable man realises his fate. He loves the child, as Socrates loved Phaedrus.

There is cholera in Venice. People begin to leave. But the authorities do their best, for commercial reasons, to hush the matter up. The exodus is slow. Aschen-bach's infatuation grows, in this desperate atmosphere, to wild proportions.

" It came, at last, to this—that his frenzy left him capacity for nothing else but to pursue his flame ; to dream of him absent, to lavish, lover-like, endearing

* Translation by H. T. Lowe-Porter.

terms on his mere shadow. He was alone, he was a foreigner, he was sunk deep in this belated bliss of his—all which enabled him to pass unblushing through experiences well-nigh unbelievable. One night, returning late from Venice, he paused by his beloved's chamber door in the first storey, leaned his head against the panel and remained there long, in utter drunkenness, powerless to tear himself away, blind to the danger of being caught in so mad an attitude." *

There is an incident, when a band of street musicians plays to the hotel guests, which deepens the ominous significance of this part of the story and points to the still slowly maturing end. The leader of the strolling players, who smells strongly of carbolic acid—the police are disinfecting the streets—and who resembles the outlandish tourist who had first sent Aschenbach on his travels, sings an impudent ballad that seems to mock the innocent foreigners. Yet, despite every warning which the novelist receives, he stays on, for the Polish family show no signs of moving. He has fearful dreams, one of a Dionysiac orgy which completes his reckless degradation. The wretched man, now more than half unhinged, brightens his dress, dyes his hair and paints his face, to find more favour in the eyes of his Phaedrus-Narcissus.

At length the day comes upon which, he finds, the boy is to leave Venice with his family. For the last time Aschenbach, infected not only by his mad desire but also by the deadly disease that is now raging in the city, goes

* Translation by H. T. Lowe-Porter.

down to the beach to feast his weary eyes. His head
" sank on his breast, the eyes looked out from beneath
their lids, while his whole face took on the relaxed and
brooding expression of deep slumber. It seemed to him
that the pale and lovely Summoner out there smiled at
him and beckoned ; as though, with the hand he lifted
from his hip he pointed outward, as he hovered on before,
into an immensity of richest expectation.

" Some minutes passed before anyone hastened to the
aid of the elderly man sitting there collapsed in his chair.
They bore him to his room. And before nightfall a
shocked and respectful world received the news of his
decease." *

This tragedy of defeat is a strange sequel to the confident heyday of *Royal Highness*. But there can be no
doubt of its sincerity. It is as though Thomas Mann, in
the full tide of his literary fame and personal happiness,
had asked himself, like a Greek philosopher, whether
any man under any conditions can ever be really called
fortunate, beyond the reach of evil destiny. The sad
and noble answer is given by *Death in Venice*. Aschenbach, the modern and more consistent Savonarola, is
only a man and must always fear the abyss, even though
he may have passed, like Plato, through sensuous beauty
to beauty of the spirit.

" For mark you, Phaedrus, beauty alone is both divine
and visible ; and so it is the sense way, the artist's way,
little Phaedrus, to the spirit. But now tell me, my dear

* Translation by H. T. Lowe-Porter.

boy, do you believe that such a man can ever attain wisdom and true manly worth, for whom the path to the spirit must lead through the senses ? Or do you rather think—for I leave the point to you—that it is a path of perilous sweetness, a way of transgression, and must surely lead him who walks in it astray ? For you know that we poets cannot walk the way of beauty without Eros as our companion and guide. We may be heroic after our fashion, disciplined warriors of our craft, yet are we all like women, for we exult in passion, and love is still our desire—our craving and our shame. And from this you will perceive that we poets can be neither wise nor worthy citizens. We must needs be wanton, must needs roam at large in the realm of feeling. Our magisterial style is all folly and pretence, our honourable repute a farce, the crowd's belief in us is merely laughable. And to teach youth, or the populace, by means of art, is a dangerous practice and ought to be forbidden. For what good can an artist be as a teacher, when from his birth up he is headed direct for the pit ? We may want to shun it and attain to honour in the world ; but however we turn it draws us still. So, then, since knowledge might destroy us we will have none of it. For knowledge, Phaedrus, does not make him who possesses it dignified or austere. Knowledge is all-knowing, understanding, forgiving ; it takes up no position, sets no store by form. It has compassion with the abyss—it is the abyss. So we reject it, firmly, and henceforward our concern shall be with beauty only. And by beauty we mean simplicity, largeness and renewed severity of discipline ; we mean a return to detachment and to form. But detachment, Phaedrus, and preoccupation with form lead to intoxication and desire, they may lead the noblest among us to frightful emotional excesses, which his own stern cult of the beautiful would make him the first to condemn. So they, too, lead to the bottomless pit. Yes, they lead us thither, I say, us who are poets—who by our natures are prone not to excellence but to excess." *

This passage from the *Phaedrus* contains the formidable thought that now accompanies Thomas Mann on the adventure of beauty to which his reading of the problem of happiness had led him. Beauty is both divine and visible, as Stefan George, the contemporary poet, was already telling his audience. It can be intuitively perceived as such. A beautiful boy may well be the incarnation of the beautiful creation of an artist. For the tree of knowledge, as Savonarola and Lorenzo, each after his fashion, had seen, is not the tree of life. But the visible leads to intoxication, excess and the abyss. The adventure is terrible and tragic and death is the end of it.

The symbols of death in this tale crowd upon the reader from the very first. The mortuary chapel, the skull-like visage of the wandering stranger in the portico, the hateful old man on the steamer, the gondolier who, like Charon, ferries Aschenbach to hell in the hearse-like bark and then disappears, the grinning ballad-monger

* Translation by H. T. Lowe-Porter.

outside the hotel, with his hospital odour, are all omens of the beauty-seeker's vain struggle against his final ruin.

The critics were silenced by this inexpugnable affirmation of mortality in a prose worthy of the great Aschenbach himself. Uneasily, after some time, the optimistically minded pointed out that the hero was less than typical. He avoided life, he unimaginably turned *bourgeois*, his fame was incredible, he was an affected self-flatterer, a hothouse plant, a cold decadent, perversely presumptuous against nature. There is no such austerity, no such inspiration, as can afford to sacrifice known experience to intuitive ideas and make a success of it.

But the archaic funeral pomp of style, with its many purples, for Mann here paints landscape with effects and to an extent he never before reached, the severe sculptural form, the incontrovertible Platonic argument of *Death in Venice*, worked out against the background of that universal solvent, the Nirvanic sea, here so exotic and demoralising, stood every literary test. The sales of the book rivalled, in time, those of *Buddenbrooks*. For some people it will always remain the best work of Thomas Mann, a classic in all the senses that the burdened but still significant word can bear, though it may be but the perfected expression of a romanticism believed to be fundamental in art as in life.

Two years after the first appearance in 1912 of *Death in Venice* Mann published in a volume entitled *Tonio Kröger* a reprint of that narrative and five other new tales.

These latter were, with two exceptions, rather slighter stories than were contained in the previous collections.

A Piece of Happiness relates how the baroness Anna, a female Tonio Kröger married to a hearty husband, finds happiness when her sporting baron's frivolous little partner, at a dance given by the Hussar officers of his regiment to some " revue " girls, kisses her hand. Baron Harry had flirted outrageously and his adoring wife was marching out of the ballroom in a passion of jealous misery when the " swallow," as the members of such touring theatrical companies are called in Germany, escapes from him and rushes after Anna to make her public gesture of apology and sympathy. It is an incident rather Russian than German. Dostoievsky would have made it deeply significant. Thomas Mann makes it carry the idea of Socrates that happiness is more in the lover than in the beloved. Anna cares nothing for the intellectual-looking cadet who silently worships her, though she is by way of being an intellectual herself. She loves, like Gabriele Klöterjahn, her gross husband, in a subconscious desire for " completion " and is delighted to find that his world can at least respect her own. Then irony enters the conception. It is easy for the simple, the naive, to satisfy their love for the sophisticated. They ask so little. But the happiness of the sophisticated lover of the naive is brief and sterile. The gulf remains eternal, the light, illuding bridge of love soon breaks down. If only one could live just on the border-line, the frontier between simplicity and sophistication ! But, alas, the beloved simpletons do not even know that such a boundary exists. The happiness of the baroness cannot last as that of the impulsive frail one will. Anna loves still, but her love can never be more than desire beating in a void. The reader finds himself again in the world of *Tonio Kröger*, *Little Herr Friede-mann*, *Tristan*, *Luischen*, and *The Famished*.

The great and perilous adventure of beauty so magis-terially recounted in *Death in Venice* is touched upon again in *Dark Hour*, a study of the creative mind of Schiller. The poet, a strange figure, red-haired, knock-kneed, hollow-cheeked, with bitter lips and towering, tragic brow, confesses his soul. The tone is elegiac. Genius is a hellish as well as a heavenly gift. It is torture for a Schiller to produce, his work is written with tears and blood. But inescapable ambition is at his back and drives him on remorselessly. It is not the deep lust for mere power of Savonarola, though Schiller can be as grim as the fierce prior in his singleness of purpose. It is a nobler, less personal longing, the passion of the artist. Sovereignty will come from the created beauty and it is not unacceptable to the poet, since it is the re-ward of heroism, such heroism as his friend Goethe will never know. For Goethe, as Schiller wrote in one of the finest of his essays, is the naive, the intuiting son of pure nature, who sings as a bird sings, without conscious effort. He may be a God, cries Schiller, but he is no hero. Goethe's tragic contemporary is the " sentimen-tal " brother, that is to say, the reflective artist, who is intellectually aware of his own feelings. Such a one must labour almost to the death, as Thomas Mann, Tonio Kröger, Gustav Aschenbach must labour, to find himself in literary creation. It is useless to attempt to combine the two methods. One is either a Schiller or a Goethe.

So far Mann, when he wrote seriously of art and artists, as he did constantly, had meant always art and artists of Schillerian, of his own type. Here for the first time he speaks of the serene brotherhood to which his great contemporary Hauptmann, for example, to name only a living German, belonged. The tale of decadence, of the quest of happiness, of the dangerous dream of beauty, would have been less grimly ironical, less passionately ambiguous, above all less practically sympathetic with struggling and limited humanity, had the writer been more Apollo and less Dionysus, approached the genius of Goethe as intimately as he did that of the hero, in a capital sense, of *Dark Hour*.

The half satirical sketch, *At the House of the Prophet*, tells the reader what was really wrong with Savonarola. The manifesto read by Herr Daniel's acolyte to a Good Friday evening audience of about a dozen people in the attic of a tenement is inhuman in its proud subjectivity. It is magnificent, but it is not a war for the world but one for a single soul. It does not represent anything common to universal experience, complains the sole sophisticated listener. Daniel, he thinks, has all the conditions of genius, loneliness, freedom, spiritual passion, great vision, belief in himself, even criminality and madness. But he has no human feeling, no human desire, no human love. The commentator himself, however, is deftly ironised, like the audience and the prophet, who does not appear in person, but is represented by a short and ugly young man with a curious mixture of brutality and weakness in his face. The piece is characteristic in its light, sceptical but kindly humour. The problems of life cannot be solved by the Herr Daniels of this world.

The Prodigy deals humorously with the riddle of the existence of a real and mature artist in a childish mind. An eight-year-old boy, rejoicing in the name, at any rate on the programme, of Bibi Saccellaphylaccas, plays his own piano compositions at a public concert. He astonishes, less by his virtuosity than by his high passion, among others a girl whom he once lightly kissed with infantile lips necessarily innocent of sexual experience. The enigma is allied to that of the Goethean poet. Beauty is produced by the prodigy in a magical way, without effort, without reflection. Again the two-sided Mannian irony refuses to take the question seriously. Here is the case, make what you like of it, he seems to say. At any rate the fact that a baby can move a greybeard through what is undoubtedly art is quite funny.

A " mill," as Tom Brown would have said, between two schoolboys is the unpromising theme of the last story in the collection, entitled *The Fight between Jappe and Do Escobar*. But Mann, as usual, gives the slight structure intellectual significance. The tale is told in the first person by a thirteen-year-old-boy of indifferent physique. His friend is the frail but bloodthirsty little Johnny Bishop, who is half English. The blond, sturdy and rather disreputable young German, Jappe, defeats the dark, fierce but too elegant Spaniard Do Escobar, in an encounter which is not half decisive and bloody enough for Johnny. It is all over in a few minutes. The onlookers are anxious for a further bout between two more champions but nobody volunteers, though the young narrator feels that he ought to. Once more it is life and art, the familiar and the strange, body and mind, which stand face to face. The artist, like Tasso, longs for life, longs to throw down his lyre and rush with drawn sword into the fray. It is not any recognisable kind of cowardice that holds him back, but the foreknowledge that the adventure, physical or mental, is not for him. The thought is related to the idea of the ultimate inaccessibility of any beauty which can be expressed by man.

The splendid achievement of the years 1911-1914 was also a curious one. In denying the possibility of the attainment of perfection by the artist, in affirming that exclusive devotion to beauty led through degeneration to the grave, Thomas Mann came nearer to creating supremely, in *Death in Venice* at least, than he had ever come before. There can be no doubt that this latter brief and pregnant study is an imperishable monument of German literature. To the native, at any rate, if not yet to every European artist, it is the apparition, expressing a mysterious grace and melancholy, which he meets on his arduous and lonely road, and which warns him, as the wise Greek warned Croesus, that his feet, however confident, are treading the edge of an abyss.

The longer *Royal Highness* had been technically exact as comedy and its argument satisfied the optimists. The tragedy of 1912 was classic and its thought, for the apologist of pessimism, could not be gainsaid. It almost seemed as though this double success in the twin fields which cover between them every mood of the human spirit was all that could now be looked for from this writer, already great, who had reached an apogee before the age of forty years. Further work could not exceed, it could at best repeat, complement or substantiate what had already been accomplished. Such is the feeling of the reader who has arrived at this point in Mann's development. Such may, even to-day, be the feeling of conservative minds. But for the intellectually inquisitive and enterprising, as well as for the serious student of literary art, an immense cornucopia of commentary and fancy, shaken by the power of the vast military conflagration of the next four years, remained to be dispensed.

CHAPTER IV
APOLOGIA AND INTERMEZZO

ONE of the masterpieces of Gustav von Aschenbach in *Death in Venice* had been a " lucid and vigorous prose epic on the life of Frederick the Great." In the autumn of 1914 Thomas Mann, seeking a medium for the expression of the thoughts that the outbreak of the European war had aroused in him, returned to his meditations on the greatest soldier ever produced by Germany. Aschenbach was a Prussian and in a literary sense a soldier, a hero who had " endured," in his favourite phrase, the service of art, which was, in its organisation, in its hardship and in its idealism, so like the service of war. His tenacity of purpose resembled that which, in Frederick, had conquered the province of Silesia, where Aschenbach was born. The character of Frederick, that savage philosopher, was of a kind, in its contradictory complexity, to attract a writer who was so deeply concerned—Aschenbach is a tolerably close study of what Thomas Mann himself anticipated becoming—with antithesis. These were some of the reflections that had led Mann to attribute a romantic study of " Old Fritz " to his last hero.

There were now other reasons why the seven years' conflict waged by the Prussian king against Europe might be an appropriate theme for a German author in the year 1914. The political situation in 1756 bore some analogy to that obtaining just before the midsummer days that set the twentieth century world by the ears. The growing Prussian State wanted room to breathe. There was a threatening policy of encirclement by Austria, France and Russia. Frederick took the law into his own hands, violated the neutrality of Saxony to a chorus of horrified protest from his enemies and marched on Bohemia.

The course of these eighteenth century events was near enough to the doings of the moment for Mann to call his essay on Frederick, which appeared in 1915, by the sub-title, *An Abstract for the Hour*. The actual name of the piece was *Frederick the Great and the Grand Coalition*, and it ran to some seventy octavo pages of lively history. The projected novel—for Thomas Mann has told the public that he had already planned a work similar to the romance attributed to Aschenbach in *Death in Venice*—had become a memoir. In other words the easy and decorative dress of a civilian had been exchanged for the girded loins and severely practical garb of the warrior.

The picture of the life and times of Frederick, the " Monster of the North," who befriended a great philosopher and forged a great nation, is vivid, economical and conscientious. The reader unacquainted with Mann's previous work might suppose that the novelist had been writing history all his life. The king himself has the double aspect of the typical Mann hero. He is, like

Savonarola, Überbein and Aschenbach, burgher in his sharply practical common sense, artist in his intellectual unconventionality. But now burgher equals soldier, and artist, civilian. The man who composed the humanistic *Anti-Machiavelli*, who loved Voltaire and kissed the lean hand that wrote *I hate all heroes*, was no mere ferocious strategist or cynical politician. Yet the contempt of a workaday statesman and martinet for eloquent theory speaks in Frederick's snarl that " if he wanted to visit a province with the severest punishment he would sentence it to be governed by writers." The enigmatic king is represented by Mann as the hero he was in actual fact ; and he is the first of the heroes of this author to be free from any touch of decadence. There was no weakness of any kind in his character. No more inspiring example of fortitude could have been hit upon for a German of 1914. The Seven Years' War " was, without exaggeration, the severest test ever a human soul has had to stand upon this earth. To stand it required such passive and active qualities, such a measure of endurance and patience, of inventive and resourceful energy, as neither before nor since, to my knowledge, a man has ever displayed or had occasion to display. Seven years long did King Frederick march hither and yon, fighting, beating here one enemy and there another, being beaten himself too, sometimes almost destroyed ; staggering erect again because he thought of something else which might still be tried ; trying it, with incredible, improbable success, and coming safe off once more. Always in his shabby uniform, booted and spurred, with his uniform hat on his head, breathing, year in, year out, the dust of his own troops, in an atmosphere of sweat, leather, blood, and powder smoke, he would walk up and down in his tent, between two battles, a dismal defeat and an incredible victory, and play on his flute, or scribble French verses, or write quarrelsome letters to Voltaire." *

No such prose, except perhaps here and there in Mann's own work, had been written in Germany since Nietzsche's time. It was worthy of its fiery hour. A patriotic German might well feel that he was repeating history, standing alone against such " decadent " foes as Frederick himself had faced. The latter had written of the French that they were " amusing asses. I like an enemy that makes me laugh." Of the Austrians what many of his countrymen thought in 1914 about the English : " I hate my grumpy Austrians, swollen with impudence and pride, no good for anything except to make one yawn." Of the Russians Mann himself scornfully noted in this essay as their chief characteristic at the date of his history a " clumsy enthusiasm." The *Abstract for the Hour* was well chosen. The nation could be confident that one of their greatest minds was loyal to their cause. As the war continued Germany at large had ample reason to confirm this impression.

There were other minds, and those far from insignificant, which were less heartening in their temper. Gerhart Hauptmann was loftily unconcerned. That did not

* Translation by H. T. Lowe-Porter. Martin Secker, 1932.

matter so much. He was a poet, a creature half child and half divinity, who contrived to remain a pure German while taking little or no part in German quarrels. But there were humanists, pacifists, cosmopolitans, " good Europeans," who were dangerous to the life of their country. They were very vocal. They called on Thomas Mann to join them. He did. But it was in armour, the full equipment of that piercing insight and deadly irony which had made him famous. He invented a name for these gentry. They were " Zivilisationsliteraten," a malicious expression which poured scorn on their rhetorical advocacy of contemporary civilisation, the rule of reason which had now once more disastrously issued in the tyranny of force.

A book of *Reflections of a Non-Political Man*, six hundred pages long, was published by Thomas Mann in 1918, but before the armistice. It is a vigorous apologia, a frank and detailed confession of his whole intellectual being, and a devastating reply to his loud " cosmopolitan " critics. Its sincerity was transparent, its fairness exemplary. Mann was under no illusion as to the quality of his opponents. The portrait which he sketches of the " Zivilisationsliterat " is bitter in feeling—these gentlemen had called Mann an " infamous, sponging aesthete "—but no caricature. Full credit is given to the foe for honesty, brains, culture of a certain sort and literary talent. This is enough armament for a critic or a journalist, but not yet enough for an artist. A certain seriousness, a certain feeling of responsibility, is still lacking. Zeal and conviction cannot be regarded as substitutes. It is a question of character, of conscience, in the last analysis of intuition.

One does not attack a phenomenon completely different from oneself. Thomas Mann shared with his adversaries such common ground as that obtaining between himself and his own brother, Heinrich, who was in their forefront. Heinrich stood for Roman, for western and southern, for French and Italian civilisation against German, to which, in fact, he denied existence. He was extraordinarily clever and extraordinarily charming. But Thomas Mann became convinced that this brilliant brother—or the " Zivilisationsliterat " he represented—was superficial and one-sided. Such people wished to absorb the Teutonic in the Latin cultures, intuition into logic. They were able, practical and in a great hurry. There was only one kind of culture for them and it was emphatically not *Kultur*, that strange compound in which emotion so improperly outweighs intellect.

The *Reflections* which sought to confute these specious highbrows had an uphill battle of dialectic to maintain. It was true that Mann had the great body of sober German opinion behind him. But nine-tenths of it was more patriotic than skilful in debate. And the humanitarians were infernally plausible, consistent and quite in earnest. At times the solitary champion of *Kultur* must have almost lost heart. What could one say to people who were so obviously bent on the amelioration of mortal intelligence? On the suppression of vulgar money-lust and stifling conventions? On the establishment of justice, liberty and benevolent peace on earth?

Only that there is a psychological principle that is more powerful than mere intellect. And this was an argument difficult to explain to the merely intellectual. The venerable dead had to be invoked in support of it. When the rationalists quoted Duhamel's *Civilisation*, that remarkable attempt to equate culture with philosophic communism, or Romain Rolland's *Au Dessus de la Mêlée*, which had just appeared, Thomas Mann referred to *The World as Will and Idea*, *A Genealogy of Morals* and *Tristan und Isolde*, that *opus metaphysicum*. He disclosed the mechanism of his own mental development, how Schopenhauer had laid down its lines, Wagner given them life, and Nietzsche speech. He laboured to prove that every one of those great shades of mighty names, valid as much for Europe as for Germany, would have understood his present position and supported his "psychological" thesis, so long as they remained true to themselves. With Nietzschean "blond beasts" and Cesare Borgia aesthetics, with Wagner's occasional and incidental hypocrisies, he was careful to explain that he had nothing to do. Rather were these lapses from grace to be attributed to his opponents, with their enthusiasm for the knowledge-worshipping moral sophistries of the High Renaissance.

Finally, Mann declared his mistrust of logical principles in general and his reliance on the intuitive processes of the mind. *Death in Venice* had been a sufficient warning against the idea of the poet as a directly didactic professor of ethics, a conception of which Plato had signified his disapproval. Abstractions are dangerous guides. The true morality is not active and propagandist, but plastic, that is, passively descriptive and critical. The true German can learn more from Russia, from Tolstoy, Turgenev and Dostoievsky, than from France and Italy. In a word, meditation, not the formation of dogma, is the proper function of the mind. Francis of Assisi is greater than Paul of Tarsus. The cell, not the crusader's camp, is the most effective nursery of the intellect.

The *Reflections* begin with a preface. Mann, in his fortieth year, which fell in 1914, found both himself and the world at a turning point in their respective histories. These essays were written to discover what was actually taking place in the Self and in the Not-self at this crisis. The environment, the early twentieth century, was less congenial to his mind in that it seemed to him to be turning back from his favourite eighteen hundreds, that honest, if gloomy, period of aristocratic romance, music, pessimism and kindly humour, to the Gallic age of reason, the time of Rousseau, Voltaire and Casanova, which he, like Carlyle, thought frivolous and insincere, with its worship of logic, sensibility, political idealism and democracy. Was Germany, any more than Mann, at home in this old-new atmosphere? It could not be so. The German stands for the abstract intellect rather than for the political intelligence, for inward culture rather than outward civilisation, for the individual soul rather than for the general sociological entity, for freedom rather than universal franchise, for art, rather than for "literature" in the sense of rhetoric. The rhetor, descended from the *sans-culotte* of 1789, has, however, attained an importance in Germany which threatens the essential quality of the German and it is the purpose of the *Reflections* to show both in their true colours.

Germany is a literally "protestant" country, as Dostoievsky called it in 1877. It protests against the idea of universal dominion, as Arminius protested against Caesar, Luther against Pope Leo X, and the modern conservative against the social democrat. But to-day there are those who protest against the protest. They are the Jacobins, the francophiles, the "Zivilisationsliteraten," the literary partisans of modern civilisation. They are determined to de-germanise Germany, to force the country into line with western notions of "progress."

Against these political orators stands the German burgher, descended from Schopenhauer, Wagner and Nietzsche, the middle term between artist and Philistine, the nationalist, the individual, incarnate in such a man as Bethmann-Hollweg, the Imperial Chancellor, whose sturdy, if impolitic, reference to a scrap of paper made such a stir in the dovecotes of western Europe.

Mann had been attacked for his championship of this figure and had been told he had set his face against truth and justice. The controversialists had attempted to con-

no whit abashed, plunged zestfully into the dust of revolution. And Mann took a holiday.

His leisure produced fruits as unexpected as ever. No post-war romance, satirical comedy or disillusioned tragedy, such as his countrymen now began to draw from the bitterness of their experience, appeared under the well-known signature. Instead, a Munich firm published, in the year 1919, a work called *The Master and His Dog*, the very title of which seemed worlds away from the contemporary atmosphere and that side of the author's personality with which his public had lately been familiar.

But this genial account of modest hunting expeditions undertaken by Bauschan the setter under the supervision of his distinguished proprietor, became immediately popular. It was translated into English four years later, the second of Mann's books to appear in the language of this country. The idyll, for it has the peaceful and remote air of that species of literary composition, though it is in prose, was an altogether new treatment of the animal theme. It was neither fable, nor fantasy, nor any kind of glorification. It was strictly objective, realistic, even scientific. Bauschan and the landscape along the banks of the river Isar are described in that marvellous idiom of Mann's which makes vivid and exact the appearance of a phenomenon never noticed before and lends a novel and striking aspect to an object which has already been perceived on hundreds of occasions. The style recalls that of *Royal Highness* in its felicitous ease and lightness. Powers of observation and of speech are here fused in the manner of the highest poetry. A fresh section of reality, hitherto neglected, is made poetically available even for those who consider dogs, in their social quality, as a confounded nuisance. Mann, detached and ironic as ever, is quite incapable of the portentous gush, the ingenuously anthropomorphic attitude which so often characterises the dog-lover in England. He knows that Bauschan is an animal and he has no illusions about canine intellectual and emotional capabilities. But he is fascinated by the zoological enigma of the setter's being and it is the love born of this attraction which has made a classic still-life of a common scene.

In *The Master and His Dog* the deeps of controversy, whether with the Self or with the world beyond it, are forgotten. No echo of these conflicts finds a way into the bright, level prose. The author appears to be merely listening, with intelligence certainly, but without much critical exertion, to the quiet but still infinitely strange music of a brief section chosen from the vast activity of life before him.

It is the same with the idyll, this time actually in hexameters, about a thousand of them, which Messrs. Fischer printed later in the year, bound up with *The Master and His Dog*. The tune is only slightly different. The beast theme is exchanged for the child motive. Thomas Mann here celebrates in not very successful verse the existence, with its various implications, of his infant daughter born against the lurid background of military and political turmoil that marked the subsidence of the great European struggle. Compared with its pendant piece this performance is not impressive. The technique is only just tolerable and the content unremarkable. The reader feels bound to note that his author, even at this late date, was capable of verse composition. And that is all. Mann could not do negligible work. But a study which neglected the *Song about Childie* would not be guilty of a very serious omission.

The next new book by Mann, a volume of essays entitled *Chapter and Verse* appeared in 1922. The contents covered the period 1906-1921 and are mostly journalism, giving a picture of his development during those years which is of interest for the study of his creative art. *Bilse and I*, the defence of judicious literary photography, was reprinted in these pages. It was followed by a frank statement of Mann's views on the theatre, no place for literature in the opinion of the author of *Fiorenza*. He can understand why the stage bored Maupassant and Flaubert. Dramatic art is silhouette, art for the masses. Both Schiller and Wagner are much more epic than strictly dramatic poets. Any literary playwright is better read than heard, even Shakespeare On the other hand a good play is unreadable because it cannot, by definition, be literature. When Shakespeare is best as a dramatist his literary merit becomes shadowy. The only chance the theatre has of being taken seriously as art is as representation in the sense of a prince's representation of his people. (This essay appeared a year after the publication of *Royal Highness*, with its discussion of princely education.) To do this properly it must recapture its soul, which is ritual, ceremony, formality. It may thus inherit the functions of the moribund official Church.

An article on Fontane (1819-1898), an old favourite of Mann's, the great balladist and composer of fine realistic novels in the French manner, notes his doctrine that style is not, as Buffon said, *l'homme*, but the permission to the objects of literary composition to speak for themselves, though, naturally, their language will be coloured by the writer's view of them. Fontane believed that the Fourth Estate, that section of a nation which is neither aristocracy, clergy, nor trading class, is the only important one from a literary point of view. He was convinced of the poetical truth of myth and saw maturity as ripeness for death. All these ideas had already found or were soon to find a new expression in the pages of Thomas Mann.

A discussion of Chamisso's enigmatic work *Peter Schlemihl* leads to the remarkable interpretation that the shadow which the hero lost, thus getting himself into such trouble with decent people who still had theirs, is intended to signify something much more solid, to wit, burgher sobriety and common sense.

The appearance of a Russian anthology gives Mann an opportunity to speak of that critical spirit which, with Gogol, begins modern literature and is the best foundation of a surer ethical sense than that of the past. An incidental judgment of interest, maintained here, is that

APOLOGIA

A characteristic eulogy of *sleep, sweet sleep* and its near relations, night, Nirvana and the sea, closes the collection.

The year 1922, which saw also the belated publication of the *Felix Krull* fragment and the first collected edition of Thomas Mann's works, excluding *Buddenbrooks* and *Royal Highness*, his two longest to date, brings for this author a period of alternate heart searching and relaxation to an end. He had explicitly and at length, for the first time since *Bilse and I*, taken the public into his confidence. He had gained from his countrymen the increased affection which such gestures create in those to whom they are directed. He had returned with brilliant success to imaginative literature. He had polished his weapons and cleared his ground for a new duel with life. No curtain descends. But the stage is set for an act that will take this great intellectual drama to a further, and a superb, level of accomplishment.

CHAPTER V

THE WORLD AND THE SPIRIT

THOMAS MANN had put Schiller in the witness-box just before the war. It will be recalled that the brief prose elegy entitled *Dark Hour* had introduced to the reader, in the romantic poet's references to Goethe, the serene contrast, as seen through the former's eyes, to storm and stress. The intellectual controversies of the war period, when Mann's " cosmopolitan " opponents had frequently invoked the calm shade of the Olympian, the sage of Weimar, the admirer of Napoleon, the " good European," had inevitably led to a profounder study by the author of *Death in Venice* of a writer indisputably greater even than the invented " classic," Gustav von Aschenbach, of a writer who had presided over *Royal Highness* and sung the songs which Mann had read in his first youth.

Goethe was unquestionably an artist. But he was far from being such an artist as Tonio Kröger, as Johann Christoph Friedrich von Schiller. These were, in Schiller's own phrase, the " sentimental " poets, the conscious and conscientious sons of the spirit striving towards nature, the world, and growing sick and decadent in the process. Goethe was the " naive " artist, the son of nature, the child of the world, who had no difficulty in representing the life of which he was already so integral a part. There were others like him, though they were very few in comparison with the Schillerians. There was Gerhart Hauptmann, who was still alive. There was Count Leo Nicolaievitch Tolstoy, who had died in 1910.

By the year 1922 the question of rank as between two such poets as Goethe and Schiller, what Mann came to call the aristocratic problem, had grown clear enough in his mind to warrant a statement. The " sentimental " type of artist had already been very fully dealt with in the books published from 1898 onwards. Mann resolved now to deal radically with the contrasted " naive." A study of Goethe alone would not have been sufficient for his purpose. The antithesis must be translated into modern terms and brought home to the revolutionary, post-war consciousness. The Russian anarchist, the only European of recent years who could be said at all to have rivalled the intellectual position held by Goethe a century before, was an obvious choice.

Goethe and Tolstoy, an essay of some forty thousand words, appeared in 1923. The superficial divergences between the mentalities of the great German humanist and the extraordinary bear-like figure, at once turbulent and pious, socialist and aristocrat, between the Olympian Zeus and the Russian god " sitting on a maple throne, under a golden lime-tree," as Gorky characterises his countryman, were shown to be negligible on a closer view. The first link was Rousseau. Tolstoy's devotion to the father of modern revolution was explicit :

" I have read the whole of Rousseau, the whole twenty volumes, including the lexicon of music. What I felt for him was more than enthusiasm ; it was worship. At fifteen I wore round my neck, instead of the usual crucifix, a medallion with his picture. I am so familiar with some of the passages in his works that I feel as though I had written them myself." *

Goethe had written at an early period of his life :

" Religious conditions, and the social conditions so narrowly bound up with them ; the pressure of the laws, the still greater pressure of society, to say nothing of a thousand other factors, leave the civilised man, or the civilised nation, no soul of his own. They stifle the promptings of nature, they obliterate every trait out of which a characteristic picture could be made." *

Again, the pedagogic and autobiographical elements in all three writers were conspicuous. *Emile* is the precursor of *Wilhelm Meister*. Tolstoy never thought of himself but as a teacher. Both the Frenchman and the Russian wrote *Confessions*. Goethe's work is of course very largely of this type. The love of self is only a particular form of the love of humanity which comes so easily to the "naive," which costs the "sentimental" sometimes life itself. Both Schiller and Dostoievsky died long before their time, sick and tormented. Goethe and Tolstoy lived well beyond the usual span allotted to mankind. Yet their

* Translation by H. T. Lowe-Porter. Martin Secker, 1932.

existences were as full of contention and contradiction as those of romantic writers. The point is that their conflicts were not the shrill, exacerbated revolts of the isolated individual against the world, against the natural order of things, but the healthy struggles of nature with itself.

The parallels grow deeper as the essay proceeds. The epic qualities of the two giant souls; the mysterious personal magnetism that made Weimar and Yasnaya Polyana shrines for the whole world, in spite of the rather stiff and cool reception which both streams of enthusiastic pilgrims sometimes encountered. Schiller and Dostoievsky were generally far more accessible. But no devotees ever blocked the roads to eighteenth century Jena or nineteenth century St. Petersburg for the sake of these " sentimental " prophets. Again, neither the Christianity nor the self-renunciation of Tolstoy is without analogy in Goethe, who depreciated his own *Götz von Berlichingen* and in his " majestic work of spiritualisation " championed Spinoza's monism. There is, further, the Russian " god's " preoccupation with death.

" It is the thought of death which dominates his thoughts and writing to such an extent that one may say no other great master of literature has felt and depicted death as he has, felt it with such frightful penetration, depicted it so insatiably often." *

This obsession is " the pendant to Goethe's intuition in the field of natural science ; and sympathy with the organic is at the bottom of both." *

* Translation by H. T. Lowe-Porter.

No solution to the "problem of aristocracy," the question which type of artist is the higher, the "naive" or the "sentimental," is proposed by Mann in this essay. But it was much to have given the point so lucid and profound a statement. So far as the idea of the artist is concerned *Goethe and Tolstoy* balances the whole range of studies from *Friedemann* to *Death in Venice*. The notion of the man of the world who is also a man of philosophic insight and transcendent gifts of expression is absent from the earlier work, unless Lorenzo in *Fiorenza* may be considered to suggest it. Nietzsche had wondered that the same man could conceive *Tristan und Isolde* and *Die Meistersinger*. But in Mann's study of Goethe and Tolstoy the Mastersinger, the artist who is also in an admirable sense the burgher, comes into his own. Hans Hansen has read *Don Carlos* and is even capable of writing as good a tragedy. Not a better one. The "sentimental" artist remains well in the picture. But the essay does mark a turning point in the development of Mann's thought, the acceptance of Goethe into the triple constellation of Nietzsche, Wagner and Schopenhauer, the recognition of the power of the world, of nature, seen now to be susceptible of as lofty artistic expression as the power of the spirit.

The striking aphorisms scattered up and down this brilliant composition gave a new splendour to the reputation of Thomas Mann. They began to be quoted, to form part of the heritage of a German's culture, even to be incorporated as so many of the sayings of his two heroes were already incorporated, in the intellectual conscience of mankind.

" For there is no conflict between nature and culture ; the second only ennobles the first ; it does not repudiate it." *

" But nature is not spirit ; in fact this antithesis is, I should say, the greatest of all antitheses."

" To all eternity the truth, power, calm and humility of nature will be in conflict with the disproportionate, fevered and dogmatic presumption of spirit."

" All national character belongs to the natural sphere and all tendency towards the cosmopolitan to the spiritual. The word, ethnic, brings together two conceptions which we do not ordinarily connect, paganism and nationalism ; thus by implication, and conversely, every super-national and humane point of view is classified in our minds as Christian in spirit."

" In (Goethe's) *Iphigenia* the idea of humanity as opposed to barbarism wears the impress of civilisation, not in the polemical and even political sense in which we use the word to-day, but in the sense of moral culture."

" Racial loyalty is aristocratic by nature, while Christianity, humanity and civilisation all represent the conflicting principle of the spirit of democracy and the process of spiritualisation is at the same time one of democratisation."

" Effortless nature, that is crude. Effortless spirit is

* Translations by H. T. Lowe-Porter.

without root or substance. A lofty encounter of nature and spirit as they mutually yearn towards each other, that is man."

Thomas Mann has a delightful way of fixing his deepest reflections in the reader's mind by the seal of a jest. The irresistible anecdote which closes a middle section of *Goethe and Tolstoy* may fittingly conclude, in the author's own style, the present notice of this study.

" They (Tolstoy and Behrs, his father-in-law) were walking about the room together in light converse, one evening, when suddenly the elderly prophet sprang upon Behrs's shoulder. He probably jumped down again at once. But for a second he actually perched up there, like a grey-bearded goblin. It gives one an uncanny feeling. I do not ask my readers to imagine Goethe, in his later period, leaping unexpectedly on a visitor's shoulder. There is a decided difference of temperament, that is clear. But the resemblance is no less so." *

The sixtieth birthday of Gerhart Hauptmann fell in 1922. Thomas Mann delivered, in his presence, a lecture which he published the following year under the title of *The German Republic*. Novalis had said that no king could exist without a republic and no republic without a king. Mann, in his graceful opening sentences, gave Hauptmann the spiritual sovereignty of the new national entity. But the lecturer then proceeded to a remarkable palinode. He retracted everything in the *Reflections of a Non-Political Man* " which could be interpreted as a

* Translation by H. T. Lowe-Porter.

defence of war. He stigmatised armed conflict between nations as a " mad rebellion against the laws of time, a psychological lie," outmoded and insignificant, a " triumph of vulgar egoism and perverse wickedness." He reproved those young people who seemed to have sworn eternal enmity to the Republic, which, he insisted, was in essence German and not French. It was this very Germanism, he rather startlingly pleads, which he was defending in the *Reflections* against the wicked Gaul. Speaking of the Americanisation disliked by the conservatives, he draws a parallel between Novalis, the German romantic humanitarian and Walt Whitman the passionate lover of the human mass. The lecture ends on an optimistic note, cherishing the break through of the European army from decadence to positivism.

The traditionalists, who had expected something altogether different from the author of the *Reflections*, did not quite know what to make of this agility on the part of their solid champion of *Kultur*. Some of them decided to be indignant. But the new attitude was merely an illustration of the fact, which should have been welcome to a patriot, that Thomas Mann, in spite of his respect for the past, his continual " backward glance," was too vital a thinker not to move with the times. He has never been afraid of the charge of inconsistency. No man has ever been better able to see both sides of a question at once and with equal penetration. To ironise the young men who were forging the new Germany would have been easy. But a master mind does not attack a mind that is still at school. It is the part of a good pedagogue to encourage it until it has reached a maturity worthy of impartial judgment. In 1923, at all events, Mann spoke, politically, for the majority.

The brief *Experience in the Occult* preceded, the following year, the publication of *The Magic Mountain*, the longest and most important work of Mann since *Buddenbrooks*. The " Experience " is a humorous but not satirical little sketch of a *séance* held in Munich, when there were mysterious " manifestations," including something like a human forearm. Mann does not decide either for or against the " spiritualists." He discusses telekinesis, the temporary, pseudo-material exhibition of energy outside the medial organism ; he talks of ectoplasm and other speculative concepts of psychic science, but as an amateur, without formulating any hypothesis clear enough to illuminate their obscurities. The piece is interesting from a literary point of view in presenting, as does *The Master and His Dog*, Mann's Goethean preoccupation with science at this period of his life, succeeding, for instance, to the philosophic colouring of his early years and the economic enthusiasms of *Royal Highness*. *The Magic Mountain*, in which a *séance* also takes place, sums up this scientific tendency chiefly in its concern with medicine.

An earlier tale, *Tristan*, had been set in a sanatorium. But that was in 1903, nine years before Mann knew anything of the luxurious Swiss institutions for the treatment of tuberculosis. It will be recalled that he visited

Davos just two years before the war. The genesis of
the great novel now published dates from 1912.

It was conceived, at that time, as a brief and playful
satire on life in a sanatorium, its puerile excitabilities, the
eroticism, the gluttony and the truculence, its craven
neuroses, the hypnotic fixations on disease and death.
The war interrupted the first drafts. But they already
pointed to a larger development. "Before the war,"
Mann tells his public in the *Reflections*, " I had begun to
write a little novel, a kind of pedagogic history, in which
a young man stranded in a morally dangerous resort is
placed between two equally eccentric educators, an
Italian man of letters, a humanist, a rhetorician, a ' progressive,' and on the other side a rather disreputable
mystic reactionary and advocate of anti-reason. The
worthy youth had to choose between the forces of virtue
and temptation, between duty, the service of life, and the
fascination of decay, to which he was somewhat susceptible." *

After 1918 *The Magic Mountain*, like *Buddenbrooks*,
began to grow of its own accord, so to speak, under the
author's hands, to the proportions of a mountain indeed.
The finished product runs to some three hundred and
twenty thousand words.

Hans Castorp, an "insignificant young man," the
scion of a family of rich Hamburg merchants resembling
the house of Buddenbrook, travels to Davos-Platz on a
three weeks' visit, in order to recover his health, which

* Author's translation.

has been slightly impaired by the ardours and endurances of his final examinations for the profession of engineering. He proposes to occupy the same institution as his cousin, Joachim Ziemssen, a soldierly youth of about his own age, who is a temporary patient in *Haus Berghof*. Castorp, compared with Ziemssen, is a typical civilian. He is shorter and slighter, and has certain mild intellectual interests. For example, funerals have always had a peculiar fascination for him, and his mind, though simple, is of an ingenuously enquiring turn. He is also susceptible to music and has a distinct taste for physical luxuries, such as very good cigars.

The honest Ziemssen does not trouble himself about such things. He is only anxious to get well and join his regiment. The strange atmosphere of the *Berghof*, elegant and sinister, makes itself felt. The pallid but robust Dr. Krokowski, the psycho-analyst, second in command of the medical staff, is introduced. The antics of an amorous pair next door to Castorp's bedroom make a disagreeable impression on the conventional young engineer. Gradually he gets to know some of the patients, for instance, Frau Stöhr, the local Mrs. Malaprop, who calls Beethoven's Eroica symphony the Erotica. Castorp's first meeting with the head of the institution, Privy Councillor Behrens, a surgeon-specialist of great repute, with an amazing conversational idiom, a sort of forced jocularity resembling a self-conscious undergraduate's, is then described. One remembers the hideous but genial tutor, Dr. Überbein, in *Royal High-*

ness. The passage is typical of Mann's method of direct characterisation and his interest in partly repulsive physiques. The style has hardly changed from the now quarter of a century old *Buddenbrooks.*

" At the door they nearly ran into Hofrat Behrens as he entered with hasty steps, followed by Dr. Krokowski.

' Hullo-ullo, there ! Take care, gentlemen ! That might have been rough on all of our corns ! ' He spoke with a strong, low Saxon accent, broad and mouthingly. ' Oh, so here you are,' he addressed Hans Castorp, whom Joachim, heels together, presented. ' Well, glad to see you.' He reached the young man a hand the size of a shovel. He was some three heads taller than Dr. Krokowski ; a bony man, his hair already quite white ; his neck stuck out, his large, goggling, bloodshot, blue eyes were swimming in tears ; he had a snub nose and a close-trimmed little moustache, which made a crooked line because his upper lip was drawn up on one side. What Joachim had said about his cheeks was fully borne out ; they were really purple and set off his head garishly against the white surgeon's coat he wore, a belted smock of more than knee length, beneath which showed striped trousers and a pair of enormous feet in rather worn, yellow, laced boots." *

Later, the cousins encounter Ludovico Settembrini, a patient who is to play a preponderating part in the book.

" His age would have been hard to say, probably between thirty and forty ; for though he gave an impression

* Translation by H. T. Lowe-Porter. Martin Secker, 1927.

of youthfulness yet the hair on his temples was sprinkled with silver and gone quite thin on his head. Two bald bays ran along the narrow, scanty parting and added to the height of his forehead. His clothing, loose trousers in light, yellowish checks, and a too long, double-breasted pilot coat, with very wide lapels, made not the slightest claim to elegance ; and his stand-up collar, with rounded corners, was rough on the edges from frequent washing. His black cravat showed wear and he wore no cuffs, as Hans Castorp saw at once from the lax way the sleeve hung round the wrist. But despite all that, he knew he had a gentleman before him : the stranger's easy, even charming pose and cultured expression left no doubt of that. Yet by this mingling of shabbiness and grace, by the black eyes and softly waving moustaches, Hans Castorp was irresistibly reminded of certain foreign musicians, who used to come to Hamburg at Christmas to play in the streets before people's doors. He could see them rolling up their velvet eyes and holding out their soft hats for the coins tossed from the windows. A hand-organ man, he thought." *

Castorp thinks Settembrini a windbag at first, as well as a hand-organ man. But later he discovers his true essence. The Italian is a humanist, a literary man who believes that the task of literature should be the promotion of the greatest possible happiness of the greatest possible number.

A second important patient, at least from Castorp's

* Translation by H. T. Lowe-Porter.

point of view, is a certain Claudia Chauchat, a Russian grass-widow whose somewhat slovenly charm makes a gradually deepening impression on the well-brought-up young man, though it is long before he has the courage to address her. She reminds him of a schoolboy he had once adored as a child and from whom, greatly daring, he once borrowed a pencil.

Castorp's originally planned three weeks pass. But he remains in the *Berghof*. He has caught a cold, has a temperature, finally is informed by Behrens that he is infected by tuberculosis and is probably in for a long stay. The news is not altogether unwelcome. Castorp enjoys the lectures of Settembrini and the proximity of the enigmatic lady from Russia. His education, both sentimental and intellectual, proceeds apace. Serious emotion awakes in him, and tries its wings. His ingenuous curiosity becomes a shrewd acumen. He discovers that Behrens is a painter in his spare time and has actually used Madame Chauchat as a model. He reads enormous tomes treating of scientific research. He begins to pay visits to the moribund, though Settembrini, in his character of humanist, does not approve of this investigation of death, in spite of the fact that Castorp's motives are as much compassionate as they are scientific.

On a night of carnival the shy young engineer at last speaks to Claudia Chauchat. He borrows a pencil from her, has a long conversation with her in French, declares his love. As she slips away to her room she murmurs softly over her shoulder : " *N'oubliez pas de me rendre mon crayon.*" The morning after this night of surrender the Russian leaves, for the time being, the *Haus Berghof*. Castorp stays on, with his cousin. Settembrini goes to take up quarters in the village, as his malady shows no signs of improvement and he cannot afford the expensive hotel any longer. The other tenant of the humble house in which he lodges is Naphta, the Jesuit and Communist, a sharp, immaculate little man, who soon begins to contradict the humanist. Castorp and his cousin are present at innumerable dialogues of great brilliance which take place between these two intellectuals. Naphta is the superior dialectician, but he is a less sympathetic character than Settembrini.

Joachim leaves at last, against the advice of Behrens, but soon returns, mortally ill, and dies. Madame Chauchat then makes a second appearance, bringing with her an aged and wealthy Dutchman, Pieter Peeperkorn, a sufferer from catarrhal affections due to alcoholism, and an extraordinary character, a " personality." He is a huge man and " talked almost continuously, though Hans Castorp failed to get his drift. Those adequate, compelling, cleanly attitudes of the hands, so varied, so full of subtle nuances, possessed a technique like that of an orchestral conductor. He would curve forefinger and thumb to a circle ; extend the palm, that was so broad, with nails so pointed, to hush, to caution, to enjoin attention—and then, having by such means led up to some stupendous utterance, produce an anticlimax by saying something his audience could not quite grasp. Yet this, perhaps, was less a disappointment than it was a conversion of expectancy into ecstatic amazement; for the speaking gesture made good what he did not say, and was of itself alone vastly satisfying and diverting. Sometimes indeed, after leading up to his climax, he left it out altogether. He would lay his hand tenderly on the arm of the young Bulgarian scholar next him, or on Frau Chauchat's on the other side; then lift it obliquely for silence, create suspense for what he was about to say, wrinkling high his brows, so that the lines running upwards from the outer corners of his eyes were deepened like those on a mask; he would look down on the cloth before his neighbour's place, and from his thick, distorted lips words of the highest import seemed about to issue—then, after a further pause he would sigh, give up the struggle, nod, as though to say, 'As you were,' and return undelivered to his coffee, which was served to him, of extra strength, in his own machine.

After the draught he would proceed thus, choking off with one hand the conversation, making a silence round him, as a conductor hushes the confused sounds of tuning instruments and collects his orchestra to begin, mastering at will any situation, for could anything resist that regal head, with its aureole of white hair and its pallid eyes, the great folds of the brows, the long whisker and shaven, raw upper lip? They were silent, they looked at him and smiled, they waited, anticipatorily nodding. He spoke.

In a rather low voice he said : ' Ladies and gentlemen. Very well. Very well indeed. Very. Settled. But will you keep in mind, and—not for one moment—not one moment—lose sight of the fact—but no more. On this point not another word. What is incumbent upon me to say is not so much—it is in the first place simply this : it is our duty—we lie under a solemn—an inviolable— No ! No, ladies and gentlemen. It was not thus—it was not thus that I—how mistaken to imagine that I—quite right, ladies and gentlemen ! Sett- led. Let us drop the subject. I feel we understand each other. And now, to the point ! '

He had said absolutely nothing. But look, manner and gesture were so peremptory, perfervid, pregnant, that all, even Hans Castorp, were convinced they had heard something of high moment ; or, if aware of the total lack of matter and sequence in the speech, certainly never missed it." *

Castorp becomes a particular crony of this prodigy, whose conversation resembles that of Jingle in Dickens or Captain MacWhirr in Conrad. The young *ingénu*, the " delicate child of life," as Settembrini calls him, listens with respect to Peeperkorn's disjointed and humourless rhapsodies, making common cause with Claudia Chauchat, who is deeply enamoured of the old Dutchman. Castorp even drags his new friend to the almost daily debates between Naphta and Settembrini. The intellectuals are dwarfed by the tremendous and yet oddly futile

* Translation by H. T. Lowe-Porter.

presence of the colossal oracle. But finally Peeperkorn
mysteriously poisons himself. He, the intuitionist, the
man of feeling, cannot survive the degeneration of his
health. For alcohol and coffee between them have at last
succeeded in altogether destroying his capacities for
sensual enjoyment. Claudia now departs for good. The
inmates of the *Berghof*, under Dr. Krokowski's guidance,
take up " spiritualism." At a prolonged *séance* Castorp
has a vision of the dead Ziemssen in the uniform of the
war of which there are already preliminary rumours, in
the garb which he had always longed to wear, and which
he would have honoured. The patients grow more and
more hysterical. There are several violent scenes and
encounters. At length Settembrini challenges Naphta.
At the meeting the Italian fires in the air, but the Jesuit
turns his pistol against himself. The European war
breaks out. Castorp leaves Davos to defend his country,
parting affectionately from the fond humanist, who speeds
him on his way. The book ends with a description of a
dangerous advance in the field made by troops among
whom the figure of the young engineer may be discerned. Whether he lives or dies remains uncertain.
But his adventures of the flesh and of the spirit have
enabled him to know, in the spirit, secrets, a " dream of
love," that are difficult of access to the flesh alone.

The Magic Mountain has the epic quality of *Buddenbrooks*. But the thought is very much more complex,
and less conclusive. For Thomas Mann has passed, in
these twenty-five years, from isolation to an intimate

communion with men. Not the single theme of decadence, but a multiplicity of themes of very varying kinds engage the closely woven texture of the novel. Yet this architecture of ideas has a common point of reference, just as a Gothic cathedral is designed primarily to exalt the thought of man to the thought of God. The synthesis of Apollo and Dionysus, of cool, practical intellect and the heat of intuition, of the world and the spirit, is aimed at from a hundred coigns of vantage.

Hans Castorp, the normal, decent individual, a sheet of paper on which anything may be written, is the theatre of this aspiration. Critics are still arguing as to whether he makes anything of it or not. The typical Mann irony leaves the decision, as usual, very much in the air. But the young engineer, as he plunges forward, with his rifle and bayonet, through the mud, in the last scene of the book, is, at any rate, a definitely changed man. His essential simplicity remains. But his horizons have retreated to infinite distances. In each of the principal characters with whom he has associated he has found something of the strange rarefaction, the equivocal quality, the apparently illimitable range, not to be found on the plains, of the air of the Swiss mountain, that air which is like the dream that takes possession of the spirit when a man begins to think as well as to perceive.

Ziemssen, for example, has an austerity, coupled with reserves of feeling hinted at in his dumb love for the pretty but seriously infected child Marusja, that is mystifying in a handsome and athletic soldier. Krokowski is genial and robust, but also pallid and more than a little slimy. Behrens' professional skill and proved warmth of heart are not free from the suspicion of a certain interested duplicity and cynicism. His jovial swagger is always felt to be forced, he has moods of brusque rudeness and inexplicable melancholy. Settembrini seems at first an ideal character, generous, clever, humorous. But Naphta's mordant sarcasms weaken, as the book proceeds, this favourable impression. There is something childishly limited, after all, about the humanist, the " Zivilisationsliterat," with his Vergilian fear of death, reaction and despots, his Voltairean materialism, his impulsive rhetoric. He is always a little the " organ-man " that Castorp had first called him. Naphta himself, the Jewish advocate of Catholicism and Communism, the contemner of life and the world, the killjoy, the bitter spokesman of annihilation, begins by seeming a horrid person. But his unanswerable dialectic, his towering invective, his uncompromising acceptance of evil, have a chill grandeur, a strange sort of heroism, which make his passionate suicide, appropriately symbolic as it is, a shock to the reader. Claudia Chauchat, again, with her paradoxical and promiscuous love affairs, her careless person and vague speech, is a far from refined character. Yet she is felt to be benevolent and even acute in an instinctive, feminine way. She sees and loves the significance of the posturing colossus, Pieter Peeperkorn, the Dutch Pan, with his elvish philosophy of sensation—" Our feelings awaken life. Man is the feeling of

God. Man is the organ through which God celebrates his marriage with awakened life "—and his obscure sorrows.

The *Berghof* is the scene of a dance of death which is also the dance of life. Claudia is the Venus of this Mount Hörsel, where Castorp-Tannhäuser stays seven years, after intending a three weeks' holiday. Time is nothing to the inhabitants. Mann discovers, before Einstein, that duration is relative. In the years prior to 1914 Europe, too, was unhealthily dancing and forgetting the ominous hours that were marching it, now slowly, now swiftly, to catastrophe. For Castorp the disaster was also the dawn. He was mature. He had begun his growth in sympathy with death, he was ending it by the determination to save life. He had turned his back on aesthetics, on Settembrini, who had fulfilled his peda-gogic function and had now no more to tell him. He was breaking through the chaos of battle to the vision of a positivist philosophy, a service of humanity, a Goethean humanism deeper than Settembrini's. Freedom of mind, he seems finally to pronounce, is nobler than death, piety of heart is nobler than life.

The tragedy, if it is one, is here not moral or aesthetic but vital. The inmates of the *Berghof* are not concerned, like Wallenstein, like the previous heroes of Thomas Mann, about their souls or their art—for there are no artists in the hotel except Behrens, and he is only an amateur—but about their lives, their humanity. Ziems-sen, is, from this point of view, their chief representative.

He has no ethical doubts, he simply wants to live as himself. The moral atmosphere of the *Mountain* is merely one of dissolution. Eroticism, for example, is rampant. It even touches the upright Ziemssen himself, though it finds no surely visible expression in him. It overwhelms the respectable Castorp. The sensual side of his love for Claudia is repeatedly emphasised. But Mann has something extremely profound to say on this subject, one of the most striking diagnoses in all the literature of love, never before so uncompromisingly stated.

" Is it not well done that our language has but one word for all kinds of love, from the holiest to the most lustfully carnal ? All ambiguity is therein resolved : love cannot but be physical, at its furthest stretch of holiness ; it cannot be impious in its uttermost fleshliness." *

Love and death, Apollo and Dionysus, the world and the spirit. Such are the generalised antithetical terms, with all their subordinate particulars, which are treated of in this last great attempt at a final synthesis. Castorp finds their musical expression in Schubert's *Am Brunnen vor dem Tore*," which he hums as he goes to his death, or a new life, on the last page of the book. The resolution of the theme is perhaps not complete. But if there is failure, the failure is so sublime that it raises the question whether success in any endeavour is not a contradiction of the conditions of human existence. *The Magic*

* Translation by H. T. Lowe-Porter.

Mountain, it is safe to say, will never be forgotten, either in its unity or in its particularity of aspect, by anyone who ever reads it.

The particularities are always vivid, symbolic and moving. They support the main structure and they are significant in and for themselves. The idea of Naphta that art is not a spiritual but a psychological organisation, that it co-exists more readily with superstition and fanaticism than with reason and conventional morality: the notion which occurs to Castorp that life is a kind of infectious disease of matter: that of Krokowski that all disease is only a transformed materialisation of the erotic principle: the views of Settembrini on the deadly, narcotic nature of the Asiatic soul, which includes charming Russian grass widows: the suggestion, of which Mann had always been conscious, that sickness stimulates the mind: these minor concepts all support the thesis that love of life and humanity comes fully only through love of death.

Such high matters are presented with a verve, an intimate ironic style continually illuminated by humour, similar to that of *Royal Highness*, Mann's other Goethean novel. The cool objectivity of the baroque story of the *Mountain* is utterly realistic, even in the lyrical passages —there is more landscape painting here than in any of the previous work except *Death in Venice*—which never become in the least sentimental. A sane, cheerful and measured tone is preserved throughout, contrasting strongly with the decadent atmosphere. The characters are differentiated with inexhaustible skill. The imaginary principals are as closely wrought as the portraits from life in *Buddenbrooks*. They are all loved by their creator, are all a part of his own inner world, even Naphta, who actually, perhaps, represents the deepest stratum. The Jesuit's fundamental rootlessness and love of dissociation recalls the destructive scepticism of Remy de Gourmont, which may be more essentially Mann than he has ever cared explicitly to admit. But Settembrini, too, is a projection of something very real in his inventor. Not even in the *Reflections* is the " Zivilisationsliterat " given so fair a field. The debates between these two champions, who talk for very nearly a third of the book, are an intellectual feast of the first order, possibly unrivalled for range and variety of content in all literature. The conversations are always, however, very clearly intelligible, for they are really addressed to the downright and unsubtle Castorp, for whose soul the protagonists are consciously fighting. The intellectual setting of the disputes is utterly impartial, even slightly mocking. No least murmur of the grinding axe is to be heard. Here is no Tonio Kröger or Gustav von Aschenbach. Thomas Mann is not singly on the stage, but he is immanent in every considerable actor, even in the miserable Wehsal —a significantly lugubrious name—whose undignified confession of his mean and hopeless passion for Claudia disgusts Hans Castorp.

Each successive work of Thomas Mann, when it is imaginative literature and exceeds the short story length, seems to be his last. The reader cannot believe that more remains to be said. It was so with *Buddenbrooks*, with *Royal Highness*, with *Death in Venice*, perhaps, in a less degree, with the drama called *Fiorenza*. It is pre-eminently so with *The Magic Mountain*. This novel gathers up into itself and expresses with a new force and developed to a new level of depth and complexity the old, disrupted, sceptical personality, the old antithesis. The " sentimental " artist faced the burgher and found himself decadent. The lonely prince discovered happiness across the bridge of love. The knight errant of beauty rode into the abyss. Now the death impulse issues in a new impulse to life. He who had in his youth resigned life here in his maturity wins it under a new guise. It seems that the pilgrimage, literary and psychological, is over. But the years that followed the publication of *The Magic Mountain* were still fruitful. And the fruit, though slight and delicate, compared with that great harvest, was full of savour and nourishment. Once more, as in the post-war period, as in the lecture on the German Republic, Mann moved with the times.

The collected essays published in 1925 under the title of *Exertions* reprinted this lecture and *An Experience in the Occult* together with some minor pieces of which the most interesting is a defence of that part of *The Magic Mountain* which deals most directly with medicine and medical men. A journalist had called it a satire in the manner of Upton Sinclair. But Mann points out that only the foreground of the book is medical. The

middle distance is social criticism, the background
metaphysical, moral, pedagogic. Death and illness are
introduced, not to satirise doctors and their methods,
but to educate Hans Castorp. Whatever effect this
apology may have had on the literary physicians who
took exception to the figures of Behrens—who was
actually identified by a lady practitioner with a real
personage—and Krokowski, with what those equivocal
gentlemen stood for, it is probable that, of all men, doctors are best able to understand the unpalatable truth that
Mann here again emphasises—it emerges continually in
the novel—that death has a ridiculous as well as an
awful aspect.

In 1926 Mann gave a lecture in his native city called
" Lübeck as a Spiritual Form of Life." The occasion
was the seven hundredth anniversary of the freedom con-
ferred by Henry the Lion. The lecture revived the old
controversy about *Buddenbrooks* and revealed in detail
the mental processes that went to the composition of that
novel. The point Mann now wishes to make is that
Buddenbrooks, and consequently Lübeck, has a reference
far wider than the boundaries of its scene. The history
of the town is a psychological and cultural history valid
for Europe, universal as well as national. That ethical
seriousness characteristic of Johann Heinrich Mann is the
personal side, Gothic architecture and the sea represent
the experience of eternity, a metaphysical dream. Hans
Castorp, with his coolness, his capacity for reverence and
his quiet sense of humour is the German middle term

THOMAS MANN

between East and West, the burgher, the Lübeckian, who remains firmly on his feet even in the strange new world of 1926, a spiritual and intellectual design for life which can never be superseded. The lecture, even discounting such elements as may be due to Mann's recognition of the solemnity of the occasion, shows how much in him still resisted the Gourmontian dissociation which had made him a Settembrini and a Naphta as well as a Ziemssen.

He was " cosmopolitan " enough, however, to visit Paris in the early part of this year and publish his extremely favourable impressions in the *Account* or jotted diary of the ten days in the stronghold of the " Zivilisationsliterat." This lively record is interesting biographically. The student of the creative artist will merely note, however, that his subject maintains his established literary standing and will turn to the fifteen thousand word story also published in this year, *Disorder and Early Sorrow*. This is a tale of the odd Germany of the months of inflation currency. The middle-aged professor of history has a particular tenderness for his little daughter, the five-year-old Lorchen. At a party, which his elder children give, a handsome and sympathetic young man plays with the child and pretends to dance with her. Lorchen is inconsolable when she is taken up to bed and " cries bucketfuls." But on the appearance, for a moment, of her debonair hero at her bedside she contentedly goes to sleep and will to-morrow, the professor reflects, have forgotten the incident.

There is no very deep significance in this charming trifle. It is remarkable for a style of masterly delicacy, for the old sure touch in character drawing and for the understanding which the fifty-year-old author shows for the eccentric new world which is growing up around him. The interest, for a non-family man, is chiefly in the adult personages, the professor himself, his servants and the German youth, which is also the European youth, of the paulo-post-war period. The natural misgivings of middle age, their resolution into humorous tolerance and a clearer perception, mingle artfully in the bright atmosphere of the tale. Yet it remains charged with a certain rueful melancholy, softening the sharper corners of the gay recklessness, but not affecting the essential sociological quality of the time, its informal impudence of a homogeneous collective unit that has said " Good-bye to All That." The sketch is a prelude, a hint at a new orientation, a touch in a fresh key.

In the year 1930 Thomas Mann published the last two volumes with which the present study will deal, one a collection of lectures and articles dating between 1925 and 1929 and entitled *The Challenge of the Day* and one a long-short " Novelle " called *Mario and the Magician*. Certain ideas expressed in the former work will be of value to the student forming an estimate of Mann's present character as a creative artist. In a lecture on the inauguration of the Poetic Section of the Prussian Academy of the Arts he notes that ever since the time of Novalis Germans had thought it natural that art and office should go together, though Liebermann had said that every artist should be his own academy. At the same time, while in France literature is a career, in Germany it has hitherto been the occupation of an outcast who tended to think any incorporation of himself into society a farce. Yet Mann himself had discovered, as he told the Lübeckians in 1926, that the poet's rootlessness is an illusion, that he speaks for many when he thinks to speak only for himself.

An article on Lessing relates the idea of classicism to that of myth through the " timeless " element in both and regrets the contemporary unpopularity of so unifying a force as that of this eighteenth century writer, who stood so firmly for the spirit against the letter, for conscience against the formality beloved of politicians. A 1929 essay deals with the theatre, which Mann had discussed in 1910 and boldly stated to be no concern of serious literary men. He reaffirms this belief in the essential childishness of stage drama, at least in the modern world, and has no sympathy with the attacks made by theatrical people on the gramophone, the film and the radio set. The death of the soul through the machine, he slyly suggests, becomes doubtful when the machine itself achieves a soul. He has no patience with the intellectual theatre which is so revered an institution in Germany. It was always a contradiction in terms and the modern " sporting " spirit is dead against it. There is such a thing as culture-hypochondria, he murmurs gently into the ears of the too high-browed anti-modernists. As for films they have nothing to do with the drama, they are epic. (It must be remembered that Mann is here speaking of the silent film only. Sound films were not yet in general use at this date.) They are epic if they are art at all. But Mann prefers to think of them as mere reproductions of life itself, of reality in the sense of the " naturalists." The fact alone that we laugh and cry so readily at the cinema but witness a performance of a play by Sophocles or Molière in comparative immobility and silence proves the point. Art does not excite noisy bodily manifestations. Life does.

Of marriage he says, with Hegel, that it is best to be quite sure that one wants to marry first, then make one's choice.

In estimating the place of Freud in modern intellectual history he finds the irrationalism of the theory of psychoanalysis, in its insistence on the subconscious, a mark of the twentieth century reaction against the eighteenth century worship of reason and traces a new romanticism in the idea of the unifying force of Eros against every species of conservative tyranny. The " Challenge of the Day," he continues in a message to the Berlin Pen Club, demands just this sincerity and world-friendliness, the transcendence of mere intellect by untrammelled feeling.

Mario and the Magician was translated into English in this same year, 1930, the year of its publication in Germany, for Mann has now a growing audience in this country. The tale is longer and solider than *Early Sorrow* and has a tragic culmination. It is recounted in the first person and reads like a personal reminiscence. The German narrator, his wife and two young children arrive for a holiday at an Italian bathing resort on the Tyrrhenian Sea. Some pleasant anecdotes of the first few days are related. Then the family go to a performance given in the local theatre by a much advertised conjurer, Cavaliere Cipolla, " a man of an age hard to determine, but by no means young; with a sharp, ravaged face, piercing eyes, compressed lips, small black, waxed moustache and a so-called imperial in the curve between mouth and chin. He was dressed for the street with a sort of complicated evening elegance, in a wide black sleeveless pelerine with velvet collar and satin lining; which, in the hampered state of his arms, he held together in front with his white-gloved hands. He had a white scarf round his neck, a top-hat with a curving brim sat far back on his head." *

This personage is, among other things, an extraordinarily capable hypnotist. He does what he likes with the audience. At last a decent young fellow, Mario, a waiter at the German family's hotel, is inveigled on to the stage. Cipolla worms out of him the secret of his unsuccessful infatuation for some local beauty. Then the magician actually persuades Mario that he, Cipolla, is the girl in question, and the lad kisses him. Amid the laughter of the audience the enraged dupe, on his way back from the stage, suddenly turns and shoots his tormentor dead.

* Translation by H. T. Lowe-Porter. Martin Secker, 1930.

The realism, the Italian setting of this grim little study in the cynical cruelty of the strong and the pitiful resistance, here finally effective, of the weak, are perfect. The reader feels that he has himself lived through an actual experience. Illusion can go no further. Thomas Mann alone among German writers has this unerring eye and exact hand. But the tale stands a little apart from the general line of the author's development, so far as it can be at present ascertained. It is the latest imaginative work of Mann. To what *magnum opus* it may be a prelude and in what sense, if at all, can only, for the moment, be conjectured.

The greatness of Thomas Mann as a creative artist is expressed principally in his genius for the delineation of human character; in his rendering of atmosphere and environment, which has the mysteriously convincing quality of the highest poetry and the most consummate painting; in his technique, with which a large and bold design is built of leisurely detail selected with and stated by the instinct of an expert psychologist to whom all the truly significant thoughts and feelings of mankind are familiar; in the acute and tender irony that permeates this whole method through and through; and in a profound sense, as deep as that of Vergil or Wordsworth, of the tragedy of life, as of the comedy which Plato, Dante and Rabelais had felt in it. He could place both on record at once in a way of such intimate communion as few but the very finest minds have even been able to imagine. The antithesis of burgher and artist, of the

world and of the spirit, that has tormented him for so
long is solved, was solved from the beginning, in his
own person, in that art which illumines a strange saying
of Socrates. Aristodemus heard it as he woke in the
grey light of early dawn, after the long banquet in
Agathon's house, among the strewn, deserted tables,
when all the guests but Socrates, Aristophanes and himself had long since left. Even the wild Alcibiades had
passed into the night, as he had burst out of it, like a
burning star. But those two indefatigable heads were
still hard at it. The talk before Aristodemus had suc-
cumbed to wine and weariness had been of love. His
brain was too sluggish to follow the whole argument that
seemed to have developed from the contemplation of
Eros. He only caught the drift of a single sentence in
his master's clear, urbane tones, to the effect that, after
all, comedy and tragedy were the same thing.

BIBLIOGRAPHY

BIBLIOGRAPHY

Der kleine Herr Friedemann und andere Novellen. Von Thomas Mann. S. Fischer Verlag. Berlin. 1898.

Buddenbrooks. Von Thomas Mann. S. Fischer Verlag. Berlin. 1901.

Tristan. Von Thomas Mann. S. Fischer Verlag. Berlin. 1903.

Fiorenza. Von Thomas Mann. S. Fischer Verlag. Berlin. 1906.

Bilse und Ich. Von Thomas Mann. Verlag E. W. Bonsels. München. 1906.

Der kleine Herr Friedemann und andere Novellen. Von Thomas Mann. S. Fischer Verlag. Berlin. 1909.

Königliche Hoheit. Von Thomas Mann. S. Fischer Verlag. Berlin. 1909.

Der Tod in Venedig. Von Thomas Mann. Hyperion Verlag. München. 1912.

Thomas Mann und sein Beruf. Von Wilhelm Alberts. Im Xenien Verlag. Leipzig. 1913.

Tonio Kröger und andere Novellen. Von Thomas Mann. S. Fischer Verlag. Berlin. 1914.

Friedrich und die grosse Koalition. Von Thomas Mann. S. Fischer Verlag. Berlin. 1915.

Royal Highness. By Thomas Mann. Translated by A. Cecil Curtis. Sidgwick and Jackson. 1916.

Thomas Mann. Von Franz Leppmann. Axel Juncker Verlag. Berlin. 1916.

Betrachtungen eines Unpolitischen. Von Thomas Mann. S. Fischer Verlag. Berlin. 1918.

Herr und Hund. Gesang vom Kindchen. Von Thomas Mann. S. Fischer Verlag. Berlin. 1919.

Rede und Antwort. Von Thomas Mann. S. Fischer Verlag. Berlin. 1922.

Bekenntnisse des Hochstaplers Felix Krull. Buch der Kindheit. Rikola Verlag. Wien-Leipzig-Munchen. 1922.

Die Gestalt des Künstlers in der neueren Dichtung. Von Carl Helbling. Verlag Seldwyla. Bern. 1922.

Goethe und Tolstoi. Von Thomas Mann. Aachen Verlag. 1923.

Von deutscher Republik. Von Thomas Mann. S. Fischer Verlag. Berlin. 1923.

Bashan and I. By Thomas Mann. Translated by H. G. Scheffauer. Collins. 1923.

Okkulte Erlebnisse. Von Thomas Mann. Alf. Häger Verlag. Berlin. 1924.

BIBLIOGRAPHY

Der Zauberberg. Von Thomas Mann. S. Fischer Verlag. Berlin. 1924.

Buddenbrooks. By Thomas Mann. Translated by H. T. Lowe-Porter. Martin Secker. 1924.

Bemühungen. Von Thomas Mann. S. Fischer Verlag. Berlin. 1925.

Thomas Mann, sein Leben und sein Werk. Von A. Eloesser. S. Fischer Verlag. Berlin. 1925.

Lübeck als geistige Lebensform. Von Thomas Mann. Otto Quitznow Verlag. Lübeck. 1926.

Unordnung und frühes Leid. Von Thomas Mann. S. Fischer Verlag. Berlin. 1926.

Pariser Rechenschaft. Von Thomas Mann. S. Fischer Verlag. Berlin. 1926.

The Magic Mountain. By Thomas Mann. Translated by H. T. Lowe-Porter. Martin Secker. 1927.

Thomas Mann, Der Dichter und Schriftsteller. Von M. Havenstein. Verlag Wiegandt und Griebel. Berlin. 1927.

Death in Venice. By Thomas Mann. Translated by H. T. Lowe-Porter. Martin Secker. 1928.

Thomas Manns novellistische Kunst. Von M. Kapp. Drei Masken Verlag. München. 1928.

Early Sorrow. By Thomas Mann. Translated by H. T. Lowe-Porter. Martin Secker. 1929.

Thomas Mann. Von H. A. Peter. Paul Haupt Verlag. Bern. 1929.

Deutsche Ansprache. Von Thomas Mann. S. Fischer Verlag. Berlin. 1930.

Die Forderung des Tages. Von Thomas Mann. S. Fischer Verlag. Berlin. 1930.

Mario und der Zauberer. Von Thomas Mann. S. Fischer Verlag. Berlin. 1930.

Mario and the Magician. By Thomas Mann. Translated by H. T. Lowe-Porter. Martin Secker. 1930.

A Sketch of my Life. By Thomas Mann. Translated by H. T. Lowe-Porter. Harrison of Paris. 1930.

Contemporanei di Germania. Italo Maione. Fratelli Bocca. Torino. 1931.

Goethe als Repräsentant des burgerlichen Zeitalters. Von Thomas Mann. S. Fischer Verlag. Berlin. 1932.

Three Essays. By Thomas Mann. Translated by H. T. Lowe-Porter. Martin Secker. 1932.

Modern German Literature. By Arthur Eloesser. Translated by C. A. Phillips. Hamish Hamilton. 1933.